MUSHROOM CULTIVATION FOR BEGINNERS.

I0136014

The Ultimate Guide To Growing Mushrooms At Home For Business, Food, Soil And Medicine

Carole Smith

Legal & Disclaimer

The information contained in this book and its contents is not designed to replace or take the place of any form of medical or professional advice; and is not meant to replace the need for independent medical, financial, legal or other professional advice or services, as may be required. The content and information in this book have been provided for educational and entertainment purposes only.

The content and information contained in this book has been compiled from sources deemed reliable, and it is accurate to the best of the Author's knowledge, information and belief. However, the Author cannot guarantee its accuracy and validity and cannot be held liable for any errors and/or omissions. Further, changes are periodically made to this book as and when needed. Where appropriate and/or necessary, you must consult a professional (including but not limited to your doctor, attorney, financial advisor or such other professional advisor) before using any of the suggested remedies, techniques, or information in this book.

Upon using the contents and information contained in this book, you agree to hold harmless the Author from and against any damages, costs, and expenses, including any legal fees potentially resulting from the application of any of the information provided by this book. This disclaimer applies to any loss, damages or injury caused by the use and application, whether directly or indirectly, of any advice or information presented, whether for breach of contract, tort, negligence, personal injury, criminal intent, or under any other cause of action.

You agree to accept all risks of using the information presented inside this book.

You agree that by continuing to read this book, where appropriate and/or necessary, you shall consult a professional (including but not limited to your doctor, attorney, or financial advisor or such other advisor as needed) before using any of the suggested remedies, techniques, or information in this book.

TABLE OF CONTENTS

✻᚛◉◉᚜✻

INTRODUCTION

꧁ↂ꧂

Are you planning to grow mushrooms? There are many good reasons to try your hand at this activity. If you want, mushrooms are a good, profitable and economically attractive commercial crop. In addition, they are easy to grow, even at a hobby level and contain important nutritional values. Some species, if that weren't enough, also boast important medicinal properties.

The period between inoculation and harvest can be very short, just three weeks. After the cultivation period, the substrate can be reused as an interesting soil improver or for composting.

The processes involved in the growth of fungi are unknown to most people. Mushroom cultivation is very different from growing plants in the garden, the processes are completely different, but at the same time, once you learn the basic concepts, nothing can stop you.

Learning how to grow mushrooms may seem complicated for those just starting out, but learning to ride a bike when we were kids seemed complicated too.

There are several techniques to learn and some specific equipment to buy, but nothing particularly complex or expensive. In any case, it should not put off those who want to approach this sector. An inexperienced person can venture into mushroom cultivation even as a hobby without having to invest heavily in equipment or expensive courses.

To grow mushrooms, the grower does not necessarily have to master all the advanced production techniques, but simply to know the right technique for the type of mushroom he wishes to grow. Give yourself the right time to learn and experiment, as indeed for everything, and it will not be difficult to master this ancient art, the art of mycelium cultivation.

One of the most complicated parts of cultivation is learning how to create your own "seed". This term is used to call inoculum, which consists of cereal grains or sawdust with the mycelium of the fungus you want to grow. It is this very "seed" that you will use to "sow" your substrate.

You will need a pressure cooker or autoclave, a supply of grains, a sterile environment, and a basic mushroom culture to transfer your culture to sterilized grains. For beginners, there are kits available where the seed has already been inoculated and is ready to bear fruit under the right conditions.

1) Cultivation using a Petri dish as a culture medium: this step involves the introduction of spores, a portion of an existing culture or a section of a chosen mushroom to clone, using a sort of

nourishing gelatin.

Processing must be carried out in a thoroughly clean environment in order to prevent possible contamination. The safest and most professional system is to use a horizontal laminar flow hood where a centrifugal fan pushes air through HEPA filters, guaranteeing sterile conditions in the working area. Since there are particles and microbes in the air that could contaminate the Petri dishes we intend to inoculate with the mycelium, these systems allow a stream of filtered and sanitized air to circulate continuously over the work area, protecting it.

Alternatively, a "glovebox" can be used, especially at the hobby level and for novice growers. They consist of transparent plastic containers inside which you can work, significantly reducing exposure to contamination by handling Petri dishes and mycelium. These containers are made with two holes to pass the hands through, often with attached latex gloves that will act as a barrier. Alternatively, the operator can wear their own sterilized gloves trying to work in a sterile environment free of drafts.

Petri dishes can also be successfully inoculated using a simple sterilized plastic container, a pair of gloves and a few precautions. The risk of contamination is greater than using laminar flow, but acceptable results can still be obtained.

2) Transfer of the mycelium in sterilized grains: this step must also be performed in a sanitized environment to avoid contamination. Simply remove a small piece of the nutritious gelatin

from a Petri dish containing your mushroom, and transfer it to a jar containing sterilized cereal. It is also possible to use a syringe with a liquid culture, which is nothing more than a liquid containing the spores that can be inoculated in the same jars containing the sterilized cereal. The fungus will colonize all the grains after a few days or weeks, and will quickly expand inside the jar.

3) Multiply the mycelium exponentially: pieces of already colonized grains can be used to inoculate several other jars containing sterile grains, exponentially increasing the production. A jar with colonized grains can inoculate another 10 or more jars containing sterile grains. The magic of mushroom cultivation is the mushroom's ability to grow its mass exponentially, reaching thousands of times its original mass. For example, a portion the size of a 5 cent piece of culture medium can colonize a 1 liter pot of sterilized cereal. A 1-liter jar of colonized cereal can be used to colonize more than 10 bags containing sterilized cereal. These 10 can be used to colonize another 100, and so on! This is what mushroom cultivation is about, this is the "secret": to multiply the biomass of the mushroom exponentially through various techniques to get to the final result, the mushroom.

4) Inoculation of the grains in the final substrate: once a sufficient quantity of colonized cereals (spawn) has been obtained, the grains are used to inoculate the final substrate, where the fungi will grow. The type of substrate depends on the species of mushroom you will be growing. Most of the substrates consist of straw, sawdust or manure, supplemented with bran and rye. Depending on the variety

4

of mushroom and the substrate used, it may need to be pasteurized or sterilized before being used.

5) Incubation: once the substrate has been inoculated, the colonization phase begins, where the fungus will grow and expand throughout the substrate in search of nutrients. When the mycelium has colonized the entire substrate, it will be ready to start producing mushrooms.

6) Induction of fruiting: In order for the fungi to begin to appear, it is necessary to modify some parameters in cultivation, placing the colonized substrate blocks in the fruiting environment. This environment, with specific conditions in terms of temperature, humidity, and light, will encourage the growth of fungi. These parameters also vary according to the cultivated species. The optimal colonization temperature of most edible mushrooms is between 18 and 26°C. Once colonized, the substrate is placed in the fruiting environment appropriate for the specific species. The change of conditions, temperature and humidity, are fundamental for some species; without it the substrate will not start producing any fungus.

7) Growth and mushroom picking: after exposing the colonized substrate to the fruiting environment, the fungi will finally begin to develop by rapidly draining moisture and nutrients from the substrate as they develop. At this point the mushrooms can be harvested and, again depending on the species, the substrate can be irrigated to allow new fruiting cycles. Some species allow multiple

collections for each colonized block of substrate.

This is a general overview of the mushroom growing cycle. In the following chapters we will see in detail every single step and everything will be clearer. My intention is to clarify as fully as possible the various steps concerning the cultivation and production of edible mushrooms, so that anyone who reads this can have a good basis to be able to approach this fantastic world.

The methods illustrated for growing mushrooms are just a few among dozens of different techniques. Each producer has their own cultivation techniques and processes, none of which are better or worse. Each technique is adapted to the reality of each manufacturer, but basically all follow the pattern described above.

CHAPTER 1
THE CHEMICAL CYCLE OF LIFE

⋟⋟⋞⊙⊙⋟⋞⋞

Nature has organized life in countless forms and ways, all apparently autonomous but independent, like the individual instruments of a large orchestra. Every living species, plant, animal or intermediate between the two, such as mushrooms, contributes in fact, with its own contribution, to break down substances.

Through successive decompositions, whatever the "thing" is, it will have to go back to being what it was originally: nitrogen, carbon, hydrogen and oxygen. Fungi, which also include innumerable microscopic species, including yeasts and molds, together with bacteria, are among the main decomposing microorganisms that mineralize organic substances. They too are part of the immense army that performs the task of decomposing plant and animal remains into smaller and smaller particles that are more easily assimilated by other microorganisms.

Therefore, they must be seen, together with other living beings, as tools that, directed by nature, allow the continuation of life. Consequently, their collection or destruction, if done in a systematic and total way, as well as impoverishing the mycological flora, could also lead to the extinction of entire species and to alterations in the biological balance.

Of the four aforementioned elements - which are the basis of life - oxygen and hydrogen are entrusted with an essentially dynamic function as fuel for organisms, while nitrogen and carbon have more complex functions and deserve further study.

The nitrogen cycle

Nitrogen is an indispensable component for plant and animal life: it is found in the soil as nitrites and nitrates and as such can be absorbed by plants, which will transform it into more complex structures to make it assimilable by animals.

The life of plants and animals therefore tends incessantly to transform inorganic nitrogen into protein nitrogen. At this point, the task of restoring the balance is entrusted to microorganisms and, more precisely, to fungi and bacteria. In the soil, microbes, through very complex processes, split the proteins of plant and animal remains first into amino acids and then into nitrites, nitrates and ammonia. Subsequently, other microorganisms will be able to transform the ammonia nitrogen into free nitrogen, which - in this form or in the salt state - will again form the soil nitrates that the plants will reuse.

However, not all nitrates will be assimilable by plants, since being soluble in water, part of them will be transported to rivers, lakes and seas. Here they will find denitrifying microbes, capable of releasing gaseous nitrogen which will return to the atmosphere. To moderate an unlimited increase of nitrogen in the air will provide other microorganisms, the so-called nitrogen fixers that live in symbiosis with plant species such as legumes.

The Carbon Cycle

Animals and plants are composed of large quantities of carbon in the organic state as carbohydrates, fats and proteins: through respiration, part of it continuously passes into the gaseous state, as carbon dioxide.

Most of it then ends up on the ground as living organic remains, and plant and animal waste, where, thanks to fungi and bacteria, it decomposes to the inorganic state of carbon dioxide which can form soil carbonates or return to the gaseous state. These continuous transformations continually enrich the soil and waters with carbonates and the air with carbon dioxide.

Through these phenomena, which occur thanks to chlorophyll and under the action of solar energy, the carbon dioxide, together with the water absorbed by the roots, is used to build the organic vegetable carbon which then passes to the animals via food. In these phenomena, fundamental to life, mushrooms play one of the primary and indispensable roles and without them the vital process would therefore be impossible.

How they live and how they reproduce

Fungi represent a group of living organisms, comparable to very atypical plants: in fact, unlike the latter, they lack chlorophyll.

Furthermore, they differ from most plants because they need to live on substances already grown by other living beings, as they are not able to process or manufacture them by themselves.

They resemble green plants in that, with a few exceptions, they have defined cell walls and, just like plants, they are immobile. Finally, they reproduce by means of spores, which can be compared to the seeds of higher plants.

However, mushrooms have no stem, roots or leaves and lack the vascular system - which from the roots carries the vital lymph to go up the trunk to reach the branches and leaves - typical of plants.

Like any living organism, they too are formed by the set of an indefinite number of cells, where by cell we mean the basic system of the structure and functioning of every living organism.

We all know a "boletus": well, the main part of the fungal body is not that large, compact, colored structure with a hat, stem, etc., which we observe and collect as a "mushroom". The main part of the fungal organism is formed by a thin and intricate network of whitish filaments, most of the time invisible to the naked eye, which, starting from the base of the stem, branch out into the soil and the underlying soil, sometimes even for several dozen meters.

What is collected as a "mushroom" is the limited and temporary fructification of that intricate and invisible network of underground filaments called mycelium, which can therefore be compared to a tree, of which the mushroom is the fruit. The mycelia form very long-lived complexes, sometimes almost perennial: in nature fungal colonies have been seen to grow continuously for over 400 years and it is likely that some could reach the venerable age of 1000 years. In theory it is possible - under ideal conditions - to have a certain production of fungi from mycelium annually.

It is therefore the set of fruiting bodies or "fungi" and the network of underground filaments or "mycelia" that constitutes the entire fungal body. The mycelium are single, very thin filaments that have a diameter between 0.0005 and 0.15 mm. (For measurements of details, in mycology, the micron, a thousandth of a millimeter is used).

The individual filaments are called mycelial hyphae, while - as already mentioned in the previous paragraph - a set of numerous hyphae is called mycelium. Ultimately, hyphae are nothing more than simple linear sequences or multiplications of cells that can, in theory, stretch to infinity if they do not find obstacles or limits to their proliferation.

They then have the possibility of dividing, thanks to particular intermediate cells, giving life to other branched filaments that diverge from the main hyphae: with this mechanism they multiply and branch in every direction. Only when multiple bundles of hyphae are reached can we begin to speak of real mycelium and finally when more mycelia merge and enlarge, we are faced with the so-called mycelial cords, already visible to the naked eye.

The mycelium then passes from the vegetative phase to the reproductive one: on the mycelial cords, clusters similar to large lumps, called thalli, are formed, which, as they grow, take the typical shape, with a stem and cap.

When the carpophore or mushroom is completely sketched out, the last act takes place: the mushroom from the subsoil pierces the ground and comes to light to finish its development and mature and then reach its real purpose, that of reproduction that occurs with the liberation of millions and millions of spores, or the seeds of fungal reproduction.

The various genera and species of fungi release the spores from an apparatus called the hymenium.

In the Boleti it occurs through the tubes which are located on the lower part of the cap, while in the Amanite and in other genera of Agaricaceae the spores detach from the faces of the gills which the lower part of the cap is always provided with.

HOW MUSHROOMS FEED

Nutrition represents the means to supply cells with "raw material", that is, with simple molecules that will be able to build more complex molecules and substances such as proteins, fats and sugars, thus forming all cellular structures.

However, the way to carry out this "refueling" is not the same for all living beings: the modalities are essentially two and the organisms are therefore divided into:

autotrophic organisms,

heterotrophic organisms.

Autotrophic organisms

Like plants, mosses, algae etc. that feed through photosynthesis using light energy captured thanks to chlorophyll and several species of bacteria that "feed" thanks to chemosynthesis using chemical energy subtracted from other substances present in the environment. Whether it is a matter of photosynthesis or chemosynthesis, these organisms are able to absorb simple mineral molecules and - with the help of light or chemical energy - build, with these elementary pieces, the large molecules of cellular metabolism.

Heterotrophic organisms

Like animals (including humans), fungi and other species of bacteria which, not being able to do as above, must find and absorb the large molecules that contain the basic energy for metabolic functions.

From what has been stated above, from a physiological point of view, fungi approach animals and move away from plants: therefore, it can be said, in a synthetic way, that they are slightly "equivocal", almost atypical plants. Modern biologists now distinguish fungi from plants, considering them to belong to a kingdom of their own, the KINGDOM of MUSHROOMS.

They appear and resemble plants, but feed and decompose like animals. In fact, their cells are not green like those of plants since they do not contain chlorophyll; moreover, glycogen instead of starch accumulates in the cytoplasm of their cells as a reserve substance, exactly as in animals. Finally, it should be added that the cell wall of fungal hyphae is not composed of cellulose as in plants, but of chitin, the same substance that forms the exoskeleton of worms, insects and crustaceans (for example, our nails are also made of chitin).

Nutrition of Mushrooms

There are three nutritional categories:

Saprophytic mushrooms,

Parasitic mushrooms,

Symbiote mushrooms.

Saprophytic mushrooms

They feed on molecules contained in dead organic material or in waste products of plant or animal organisms. They can also be classified regarding:

Soils: they live exclusively at the expense of humus;

Lignicolous: they live on branches, trunks, dead stumps and even on worked wood;

Cinericoli: they live on remains of wood or other charred material;

Coprophils: live on animal excrement and manure;

Necrophils: live on dead animals.

There are even more specialized species in the world of

saprophytic fungi, which live in different habitats such as dead leaves fallen to the ground, fallen needles and pine cones of conifers, on other decaying fungi etc.

In all these cases the fungus represents the first step towards its total disintegration and transformation into humus, of the organic material accumulated on the ground, thanks also to the help of some bacteria and other components.

Parasitic Mushrooms

They feed exclusively on material contained in other living organisms. Parasitism is often lethal to the attacked beings. In some cases, from primitive situations of pure parasitism, through intermediate phases, a "balanced" situation of mutual exchange of material between fungus and host is reached. In this situation, we speak of symbiosis (see next point), of which lichens are an example, the result of symbiosis between a fungus and an alga, or mycorrhizae, symbiotic bonds that are established between a fungus and a plant. Finally, some fungi begin their activity as parasites and when the host plant dies they continue their existence as saprophytes until they completely consume all traces of the host plant.

Symbiote mushrooms

Among the various interactions that occur between organisms in a natural environment, the most perfect is undoubtedly the mutualistic symbiosis. Symbiosis, which in this case finds its typical expression with mycorrhizae, is the life in common that is expressed between the fungus and the tree, where the hyphae of the fungal mycelium attach and envelop the radical extremities of the plant with which the fungus will live.

This symbiosis allows a useful exchange of substances between the two organisms, in which the fungus absorbs from the plant the organic substances that it cannot synthesize due to the lack of photosynthetic pigments, while the plant having - thanks to the mycelium - increased its root surface, will be able to absorb to a greater extent water, mineral salts and other substances useful for its own growth, much further away from its real roots, thanks to the mycelium web that is much more extensive than its root system.

Let's go deeper into the mechanism of symbiosis.

The spores of a symbiotic fungus that have accidentally fallen into soil - made particular by the special root secretions of the plants, composed of organic acids, amino acids, salts etc. - are urged to germinate and give rise to the fungal hyphae, which, growing and swelling, will then form the mycelium.

At this point, the capture of the hyphae by the plant takes place, thanks to particular chemical references. Therefore, the roots of the plants, with their secretions, attract the hyphae and these envelop them forming around them a thick felted tissue called mycoclena; at this point, the only possibility left for the plant is to feed itself by passing through the hyphae and mycelia of the fungus.

Thus, the mycorrhization has been completed and the symbiosis is now in progress. This process could suggest that the plant has to suffer, but, instead, it will greatly benefit, to the point that many forest essences can take root - in certain particular soils - only if combined with mushrooms.

Through the phenomenon of fungal symbiosis, the plant receives, through the mycelium, water and mineral salts.

Thanks to the phenomenon of chlorophyll photosynthesis, the plant captures solar energy and transforms it into chemical energy, thus synthesizing sugars, amino acids and proteins.

These elements descend through the branches and the trunk to the roots from which the fungus draws its nourishment.

In summary, this is the functional, structural and, so to speak, almost "affective" link between plant and fungus, known as symbiosis.

CHAPTER 2

GENERAL NOTIONS TO START

MUSHROOM CULTIVATION

N ow that we understand what mushrooms are, let's see how we can grow them.

But we'll also look at how a successful profitable mushroom cultivation business can be built and what are the best mushrooms to grow both for ease and for the profit they can bring us.

Mushroom cultivation is very simple. Start by choosing among the many varieties which to grow.

The mushrooms to be cultivated are sold in various ways: as dissolved mycelium or a block containing the spores that will be useful for the cultivation of the mushroom.

Once you have chosen the type of mushroom to grow, you can move on to preparing the soil, which must be quite moist and rich in organic substance. In fact, even garden soil can be fine, as long as it's not too acidic.

Mix horse manure or slow-release organic fertilizer into the soil. Mix carefully to form an even blend; finally wet the soil a little and let it rest for 5 days. Then you can place either the block or the free mycelium in the soil.

In the first case, cut the bag lengthwise, placing it on the ground and leaving the plastic on the underside.

In the second case, place the mycelium in a plastic bag that will have to be put in a hole 20-30 cm deep, in this case I suggest you place the soil in a fruit and vegetable box.

Then water lightly and cover both block and mycelium with the soil. Water the substrate every day, being careful not to create stagnation of water, also let the substrate remain at a temperature higher than 10°C. After 15 days you can already pick your mushrooms; if you want to regenerate the soil, all you have to do is turn it.

Grow mushrooms with a kit

There are many kits on the market to grow mushrooms quickly and easily. These kits can come in very handy if you want to grow mushrooms with your kids, then use that as a game or if you just don't have a green thumb or a lot of time to grow mushrooms.

A kit generally contains everything you need, from the spores - which in this case have a very fast growth process - to the soil, any soil - from the most common one to coffee grounds.

Obviously, each kit has a different method of use, but generally when you buy the kit you will have to extract the bag with the spores from the package; immerse it in water for a few hours; place the spores inside the package where the soil will be; place the former in a recommended place at the right temperature and moisten the spores regularly. After a short time you will have your mushrooms ready.

Methods for growing mushrooms

The methods for growing mushrooms are varied, also because they can grow on any soil and at an impressive speed, as they are molds.

Mushrooms can be obtained from cultivation in a box, but they can also be grown through kits as we have already seen.

Curiously, mushrooms can also be grown using toilet roll tubes.

To grow mushrooms like this, all you have to do is moisten the tube in boiling water with the heat off and then place it with the spores inside a bag.

Finally, leave this bag to ferment for 3 weeks in a dark and sufficiently humid environment. Then refrigerate the bag for 48 hours to speed up the growth process.

Remove the bag from the refrigerator and the roll from the latter, then leave it to rest at room temperature, in a lighted place, wetting it regularly using a sprayer.

After 7-10 days the mushrooms will be ready to be picked.

How to start a profitable mushroom farm

Certainly, starting a business is not easy, but starting one with mushroom growing at the center could prove to be very intelligent, especially since this activity is niche, therefore also highly sought after.

I strongly advise you to think big and start with small investments, and then enlarge your production; I therefore intend to advise you to start with a small greenhouse and focus not on the size of the production, but on possible customers.

Try to make yourself known and then expand your production through customer loyalty. Make your company feel like a family by organizing various initiatives such as educational visits or informational tours. Thanks to these, the customer will become familiar with your company and your product will be increasingly in demand.

The easiest mushrooms to grow and the most profitable ones

Mushrooms are divided into two large families: saprophytes and symbiotes. It is much easier to cultivate the former. Champignon mushrooms are very easy to grow, and are also among the best sellers, as are the chiodini, and pioppini mushrooms, which are already more difficult to see on the market.

You can also grow the stropharia variety and the more oriental shiitake.

There are also many mushrooms that, if cultivated, could prove to be profitable, among these there is always the champignon which sells well and which could prove to be an excellent investment not only because it ensures a very high production, but also because it does not cost a lot.

To have a profitable crop, you could also think about a cultivation of pleurotus, which are much more difficult to grow than champignons. Don't lose sight of the new trends that could prove to be very fruitful, so you could also grow charcoal, pioppino and shiitake, but also the so-called golden mushrooms and love mushrooms.

If you want to grow mushrooms but you are not a real expert, try growing champignon mushrooms, which are the simplest among the various species.

Growing mushrooms has been known since ancient times. The reason? Simple, because mushrooms have always represented a popular and sought-after dish, and the cultivation of mushrooms was the practical solution to this need.

In fact, saprophytic fungi use dead organic substance for their growth and reproduction. This fact makes them particularly suitable candidates for both greenhouse and home growing.

Bales of freshly fruited mushrooms

In fact, in the artificial cultivation of mushrooms, all that is done is to provide these saprophytic mushrooms with the nutrients they need to grow and to complete their life cycle, in an artificial environment or in an artificial mushroom farm or mushroom greenhouses.

Obviously, not all saprophytic mushrooms are suitable for cultivation at home in greenhouses or in artificial mushroom beds. However, some of them manage to produce the fruiting body.

The most distant news that bring us back to the topic of cultivated mushrooms dates back to two centuries before the Christian era and concerns the Greek Nicandro, a doctor and scholar who taught how to grow mushrooms at home. Nicandro cultivated mushrooms inside some holes full of manure specially dug near some particular trees. In these holes, Nicander kept the humidity suitable for the development of fungi.

We also know of another Greek doctor named Dioscorides who reported the fact that Romans and Greeks used the cultivation of mushrooms with special litter filled with soil mixed with manure. The mushrooms grown at home were the piopparelli mushrooms (pholiota aegerita) and crushed poplar bark was also mixed into the substrate.

The physician and botanist Andrea Cesalpino, around the mid-1500s, took up the ancient methods of producing cultivated mushrooms.

More recently, the practice of growing mushrooms has spread radically.

In Japan, growing mushrooms is a practice that goes back thousands of years. For example, the Tricholomopsis Edodes is a particularly popular mushroom for cultivation. Growing Shiitake mushrooms in Japan involves preparing the mycelium.

In general, all saprophytic fungi can be cultivated. The problem lies in finding the right procedure for each individual species. These procedures then, once found, must also be economically sustainable.

Pleurotus mushrooms, on the other hand, can give excellent results even in cultivation at home and by now the procedure for their cultivation is well established.

The agaric mushroom, on the other hand, requires more complex structures than the living room of one's home. Cultivating mushrooms has therefore become a common practice and has also aroused the interest of the industry since the necessary substrates are composed of cheap materials and the selling prices of mushrooms grown at home are characterized by attractive prices.

The substrate for growing mushrooms is an organic compound made from wheat straw, barley straw, rice straw, corn straw or wood and bark residues. We will see later how to create it by hand or where to buy the substrate.

Yellow wheat straw should be cut into pieces of 2-3 cm and watered for 24-48 hours, mixing abundantly, to moisten all the strands of straw. Then it must be drained and mixed with the mycelium. Once this is done, the mixture is put into 5-10 liter plastic bags and the bag is closed, but not sealed, as air must pass through.

Once it is ready and inoculated, just wait 3-4 weeks leaving it in the greenhouse at 25-28 degrees and all the straw will be covered with mycelium.

We have already said that mushrooms are an organism that do not need sunlight to grow. In fact, they can grow in dark areas, where however the humidity is right for their development. That is why it is often recommended to place mushroom bales in dark and damp cellars.

If you want to do something more professional, you could set up some greenhouses for mushrooms, to be able to grow large quantities of crops on your own.

A mushroom greenhouse made with plastic and fans for air circulation.

Conditions of the Mushroom Greenhouse

If you have a greenhouse available, you may need to shade it or otherwise modify it to block out the sunlight. Another necessary measure to take is the temperature. It must remain stable around 16 degrees. The air must also remain humid and the environment must be protected from any drafts that can block the development of the mushrooms.

Which mushrooms to grow?

Pleurotus mushrooms are among the easiest to grow. They grow fast and can be harvested only 7 days after the carpophore grows out of the bales. The full growth cycle lasts only 3 to 4 weeks and therefore several harvests can be produced each year.

Growing shiitake mushrooms is also quite easy and they can be sold at a great price.

Even from the point of view of the necessary space, the cultivation of mushrooms (fungicultura) does not have particular needs. In fact, even small spaces can be used.

STEP 1: Find the right place

We have said that growing mushrooms indoors does not require particularly demanding places of size. In reality, the mushroom growing process is divided into 3 distinct phases, each of which requires a different space.

The 3 stages of mushroom farming are actually the three stages of the mushroom growth process, and they are these:

Inoculation

This is the stage where the mushroom spores mix with the mushroom substrate. The mixture thus obtained is packed inside bags called "mushroom bales". Step 1 simply requires a comfortable space to inoculate the substrate. So you just need a workbench or shelves that can then be cleaned easily. You also need a vessel to mix the spores with the substrate.

Incubation

At this stage the bags filled with mushroom substrate inoculated with the spores are left in a dark and warm place to allow the mushroom mycelium to grow and expand throughout the bale. This phase requires a closed place where a temperature between 20° and 24°C can be maintained.

Bales of inoculated mushrooms incubating on shelves.

It could also be a shaded or darkened mushroom tent or greenhouse that you can build with wood or metal tubing. It could also be a metal shipping container or a garage. The bales of mushrooms must be arranged on the shelves, neatly. Or you can also hang them from metal bars fixed at the top.

Fruiting

This is the moment when the mushroom bales are opened or cut and the mushroom substrate is exposed to air and humidity, stimulating the growth of the carpophore body of the mushroom, which is the fruit we will harvest. This phase requires an environment that is more difficult to recreate than the previous two phases.

PHASE 2: Construction of the Mushroom

Obviously, you have to build a room for the fruiting of mushrooms considering the volumes and quantities of mushrooms that you want to produce. There must certainly be shelving. It will also require electricity and access to water as well as the installation of some kind of system that brings air in and out of the mushroom farm.

Garages, cellars or even metal containers can be used to grow mushrooms as well as a mushroom greenhouse. In general, it takes about 10-20 square meters to produce 50 kg of mushrooms and it takes 10-15 hours of work per week to harvest 10 kg per week.

Greenhouses can be built inside large rooms, setting up a frame with wooden strips and lining everything with nylon or plastic sheets. This is definitely an inexpensive option.

PHASE 3: Cultivation begins

Now that we have everything ready it's time to start working on mushroom growth. The method we like best is the one that involves low energy consumption. We have already explained you can make the substrate with straw, or for example, with coffee grounds. In this way, already pasteurized ingredients are used. Straw and sawdust are also used but usually the sawdust should be brought to a high temperature to eliminate bacteria and all other organisms that we do not need, and that could compete with our fungi.

We then mix the straw, sawdust and coffee grounds in our inoculation room to get our substrate and pack it into the mushroom bales.

We must be careful with the proportions of the ingredients. They should be weighed before mixing, for example 1.5 kg of coffee grounds can be mixed with 300g of sawdust and 150g of Pleurotus Ostreatus spores. Oyster mushrooms are the easiest to grow and give the most abundant harvest.

PHASE 4: Collection and sale of Mushrooms

Now, if all went well, you will have waited 2-3 weeks for the mushroom mycelium to branch well into the substrate during incubation (at 20-24°C) You will have opened the bags with a cut, in the room that has constant humidity and fresh air, and see mushrooms sprouting that every day double in size. The time has come to collect them and to be able to enjoy the fruits of your own homemade mushroom farm.

CHAPTER 3
THE MYCELIUM FOR CULTIVATION

I f you need to study the mycelium, you can produce it yourself in spring or summer by following these steps:

First of all, you need to fill a tray or pot - with holes in the base - with a new substrate.

Then, water it so that it is well wet.

Then place the spores on the substrate.

Finally, place the tray or pot in an area with little light and spray the substrate with water to keep it moist.

This is the ideal option, but if you have a plant that has been watered too much, it may or will soon have mycelium somewhere on its body.

How long does the mycelium last?

If done in the laboratory, under controlled conditions, Morelas can take a day while Agaricus a month to cover a Petri dish, which is a low, round shaped glass or clear plastic container (about 2 centimeters) and a diameter of about 5-7 centimeters which is used to cultivate and study the behavior of different microorganisms.

When breeding most mushrooms, the mycelium of cereals, purchased on special farms, is used. To grow mushrooms, the mycelium must be stored under certain conditions, and before planting it is necessary to check its quality. But, even with excellent planting material, one cannot do without special substrate preparation - it requires heat treatment and sterilization.

Currently in mushroom cultivation, oyster mushrooms and shiitake predominantly use vegetative sowing with the help of the so-called sterile grain mycelium. Non-sterile wheat mycelium for growing mushrooms at home is not used, because under non-sterile conditions, wheat is quickly affected by putrefactive bacteria and mold. The mycelium of cereals is suitable for the reproduction of most mushrooms. The grains of wheat, barley and millet produce mycelium of oyster and shiitake mushrooms, the grains of wheat and rye - mycelium of champignons and donut. Mushroom growing cereal mycelium has a good supply of nutrients. Mycelium produced by a large company, as a rule, guarantees the successful cultivation of the mushroom that is indicated on the package.

The mycelium of cereals is sold in plastic bags with an air filter containing 8 kg of mycelium. The filter is needed for oxygen and to protect the mycelium from molds and other competitors. With improper storage, the mycelium of champignons and most other mushrooms die when the air temperature rises above 30°C. And at a negative storage temperature, the mycelium freezes and loses quality.

Long-term storage of mycelium for oyster mushrooms and other mushrooms is allowed at an air temperature of 2°C. Packages should be packed at intervals, as the mycelium is heated due to its own living. At home, storage of wheat mycelium is possible in a home refrigerator, but not in a freezer. It should be borne in mind that, in modern domestic refrigerators, the storage of mycelium, although allowed, in a chamber with automatic defrosting, the temperature periodically varies from 1 to 10°C. Thus, with a long shelf life of mycelium and oyster mushroom, a hard mycelium crust and the beginnings of fruiting bodies are formed inside the package, and the mycelium of champignons and annulus quickly deteriorates.

When buying mycelium in small packages, you need to make sure there is an air filter or holes in the airbag. Without this, the mycelium will decompose quickly and with filter-less holes, sooner or later it will attract mold.

Even if you have complied with all the conditions of storage of the mycelium of mushrooms, before planting, you need to check its quality. You can do this in the following way. Prepare a solution of one teaspoon of sugar in a glass of boiled water. Fold the toilet paper into several layers with a 5x5cm square. Clean toilet paper is sterile, unlike wipes. Moisten a square of paper with a sugar solution, squeeze it and place it in a petri dish or on a clean saucer. Place a few grains of mycelium in the bag you purchased and cover with a lid of a petri dish or glass. At room temperature, a week later, on a grain or other substrate sold as mycelium, a white fringe should appear from the mycelium growing in the air. There should be no color spots. This mycelium sprouts and a few months later should not have mold spots. So you can check not only the grain, but also any other mycelium.

Reproduction of mycelium of oyster mushrooms and other mushrooms at home

Purchased high-quality mycelium can be independently propagated. To multiply the mycelium of mushrooms, the wheat grain must be boiled over low heat for 20-25 minutes. It is important that the core of the grain remains white. Then the grain must be dried on a table, mixing it with a spatula for 30 minutes. It can be dried under a fan. After that, it should have a humidity of 50-53%. For drying, gypsum can be added to the grain - 5%, by weight, of the grain. Thus the prepared grain is poured into two-liter glass jars at the rate of 1 kg per jar. Wheat when breeding oyster mushroom mycelium at home, should occupy less than half the volume of the pot. A hole with a diameter of 3cm is made for the cork stopper in the center of the lid. To prevent boiling water from getting the cotton stopper wet, wrap the lids with aluminum foil or kraft paper, which you tie around the neck of the vase with string. Trim the excess off the paper.

When the mycelium propagates, put a rag under the cans and pour cold water to 3-4 cm below the lids. To sterilize the grain, the jars need to be boiled twice for 2 hours at one-day intervals. In the interval between boiling, they should be at room temperature. When using an autoclave at a temperature of 120°C and a pressure of 1.0

atm. it is sufficient to sterilize once for 2.5 hours. Domestic autoclaving at 110°C is also acceptable.

Without removing the lids, the wheat jars must be cooled to 22 - 55°C and transferred to a sterile box or other clean room for sowing wheat with sterile mycelium at your disposal. During planting (inoculation), the lid with the filter must be removed, put a spoonful of mycelium in the jar and close the lid again with a cotton plug, then with kraft paper and tie. Then the jars need to be shaken to evenly mix the mycelium with the grain and put them in a clean room with an air temperature of 24 - 26°C for overgrowth.

The incubation time in the pot with grain is 14 days for the reproduction of the oyster mushroom mycelium and more than 30 days for the shiitake. The duration of the incubation of other mushrooms takes the same period. After 7 days of mycelium growth, the contents of the cans should be shaken so that the grain is not too tight from the mycelium and the overgrowth of the grain is uniform.

After the grain is completely overgrown, you can transfer the mycelium from the cans into plastic bags.

Substrate for the cultivation of oyster mushrooms and other mushrooms

Good yields of oyster mushrooms, shiitake and other mushrooms can be grown on a loose substrate made of shredded straw, cotton tow, sunflower husk, or ground twigs. Nutrient additives can be added to such a substrate for growing mushrooms and heat treatment

34

of the substrate will free it from mold. The granular structure provides oxygen access to the developing mycelium, so the development of such a substrate occurs many times faster than the development of dense wood. To create a high concentration of carbon dioxide, which is necessary for the growth of the mycelium, the substrate in the house is placed in plastic bags with air-permeable caps or with perforation.

The substrate base is called the material, which comprises more than 50% of its total mass. The nitrogen content in the basic materials of the substrate is as follows: sawdust - 0.1%, linen - 0.5%, straw - 0.6%, husk - 0.7%, cotton tow - 0, 7%, ground branches - 0, 7% (all in relation to dry weight). To obtain the optimal nitrogen content (0.7-1.0%), the substrate for mushrooms can be made by adding grain or bran to the amount of 10-20% of the dry weight of the substrate. The substrate must be moistened in such a way that its moisture content is between 45 and 70%. The optimum moisture content of the substrate is 60%.

The moisture content of the substrate for mushrooms (W%) is the percentage ratio of the mass of water in it to the mass of the substrate. The humidity is determined as follows: 100 g of substrate are stored in an oven for 6 hours (constant weight) at a temperature of 110 - 120°C (not higher than 150°C to prevent carbonization of dried components).

The difference between the weight of the wet and dry sample, expressed in grams, will be numerically equal to the moisture content of the substrate as a percentage. You can dry a 100g sample in a microwave instead of an oven. Set the microwave oven at a level of 350-400 watts. Heating mode: heating 4 min; break 2 min; warm-up 4 min; break 2 min; 4 minutes of warm-up.

Fungi - aerobic organisms that consume atmospheric oxygen and emit carbon dioxide. Therefore, the main parameter of the substrate base for fungal mycelium is its air permeability: the substrate structure must be free and the substrate block shell (plastic bag) must have an opening for "breathing". The permeability of the moist substrate for air decreases dramatically as the particle size of the substrate base decreases and, especially, when the substrate is flooded with water, when areas filled with free water appear. The diffusion coefficient of oxygen in water is tens of thousands of times lower than in air. Thus, the over-hardening of the substrate for oyster mushrooms and other mushrooms creates anaerobic conditions, in which the mycelium cannot exist.

Processing when preparing a substrate for mushrooms at home

The best material for the future substrate mycelium is the small fragments of ground fresh deciduous branches. If it is not possible to use all the prepared raw materials at once, then you need to grind the branches and then dry at a high temperature in the oven. From 1000 g of fresh branches, 500-600 g of dry branches will come out. Instead of branches, you can use shredded straw, flax, or sunflower seed husk not exposed to rain. The next step is to prepare the right amount of clean three-liter jars. Make a 1-2 cm round hole in the lids of the plastic cans. Wash the lids and cans thoroughly. Firmly insert sterile cotton plugs (twisted pieces of cotton wool) into the plug holes. At the time of heat treatment of the cans, remove the lids with corks in a clean plastic bag.

After preparing the substrate to the amount needed to fill one or more three-liter containers, transfer it to jars filling to a few centimeters below the neck. Pour boiling water into the substrate in the jar slowly, so that the jar does not explode. After absorption, add boiling water so that it completely covers the substrate. Close the jars with lids with holes to drain the water, but do not immediately drain the water. Let the jars cool slowly at room temperature for 2-3 hours, turn the jars upside down, drain the water from them and leave them upside down for a day. During this time, the water will drain from the cans and the dead spore mold in the substrate will germinate and become defenseless due to a repeated rise in temperature. This method is called fractional pasteurization of the substrate.

In the process of preparing the substrate at home, weigh each balance of moistened contents. For heat treatment of the substrate for oyster and other mushrooms, close the jars with aluminum foil or a tin lid. Put the jars in any thermal oven for 3 hours at a temperature of 80°C.

Let the jar cool to room temperature and weigh it again. If the can with the substrate has lost more than 20% by weight during heat treatment, bring the mass of the can to 80% of the original by adding boiled water to the substrate. Remove the aluminum foil and close the jar with a clean polyethylene lid with a cotton cap. The substrate is now ready for inoculation with its mycelium.

An easier way to heat the substrate is called xerothermic. What follows is the preparation of a substrate soaked in the desired moisture content in the amount needed to fill one or more three-liter cans. Put it in jars.

Seal the substrate so that it does not reach the neck by a few centimeters. Weigh the jars with the substrate. Put the cans in the oven, heated to 110°C for 2-4 hours, to boil all the water from the substrate, cool the cans and fill the substrate with clean boiled water in such an amount as to restore the weight of the substrate that was there before heat treatment. Close the jar with a clean polyethylene lid with a cotton cap. The substrate is now ready for inoculation with its mycelium.

Processing the substrate of oyster mushrooms and other mushrooms in the garden

With a clean, mold-free raw material, pasteurization can only be done once. In the garden, you can pasteurize the substrate in a 200-liter barrel. Place the barrel on concrete blocks or bricks. Pour 50 liters of water into it. Above the water, on bricks arranged vertically inside the barrel, insert a round (barrel-shaped) net or grid.

Having prepared the substrate for the mushrooms of the desired composition and humidity, put it in polypropylene bags, leaving part of the bag empty to tie with a rope. Low pressure polyethylene "rustling" bags can be used. More elastic bags made of high-pressure polyethylene, which do not rustle, are not suitable for this. They will collapse after boiling. More expensive bags designed for freezing food are also suitable. Insert a cotton ball or winter synthesizer into the throat of the bag like a breathable plug. Pull the throat of the package around the cap with the string. Place the substrate blocks in different levels on the cork grid. Close the barrel with a lid and leave the barrel with the substrate for a day or more for mold spores to grow in the substrate. The next day, light a fire under the barrel and boil the water for 6 hours straight. By the next morning, the substrate in the barrel will cool down. To "inoculate" the substrate, dissolve the bag, remove the cork, check that the temperature of the support is below 30°C, add the mycelium, then reinsert the cap and tighten the throat of the bag with string.

When growing mushrooms such as shiitake or maitake, for greater reliability, double fractional pasteurization is required. The sequence of operations for the double fractionated pasteurization is as follows. Bags with a substrate soaked in the required moisture, closed with a synthetic winterizer or cotton swab, are stored at room temperature for 24 hours, then placed in a "Chinese barrel" on a fire, pasteurized at a temperature of 80 - 100°C for 3-6 hours, depending on the volume of the bag. Subsequently, they are left to cool in the barrel for 16-24 hours, then a fire is lit again and a second pasteurization is carried out.

Similarly, pasteurization can be carried out in a sauna or any other bath at 80 - 90°C.

Substrate preparation for oyster and other mushrooms: sterilization

The base of any autoclave is a sturdy container with a lid that resists the excessive pressure of the water vapor inside and is equipped with a valve for steam purge in case of dangerous pressure. It is believed that when preparing a substrate for oyster mushrooms and other mushrooms in an autoclave, complete sterility is achieved at 134°C - all known organisms on earth die. Microorganisms that can damage cultivated mushrooms die at 120°C. Industrial autoclaves intended for mushroom cultivation operate at an overpressure of 1 atm, which guarantees the treatment of the substrate at 120°C with "flowing steam". This allows you to completely sterilize the substrate for mushrooms.

A few words about what the "fluid vapor" treatment is. From the steam generator, the steam is fed into the autoclave tank, where the substrate is in open containers or in sealed bags. Part of the steam can be purged periodically, ensuring that new steam enters the autoclave. This wet substrate treatment provides complete sterilization. In this case, all sections of the substrate are treated with steam and not dry air. This is very important, since the dry spores of some molds and bacteria remain viable at a temperature of 160°C.

Currently, online stores offer various home autoclave options designed to sterilize canned food at home. They are similar to our "Chinese barrel", but work with high pressure steam, providing the processing of canned food or, in our case, the substrate at a

40

temperature of 110°C. Bags or jars with a substrate are placed inside a domestic autoclave on a rack over boiling water. This is not a "flowing steam" treatment and not a complete sterilization of the substrate, but this treatment is sufficient enough to grow mushrooms in a private household.

The selected substrate must be mixed in a basin with any additives and with water in the quantity necessary to reach the required humidity of the substrate. Transfer the substrate into packets. Close the bags with cotton or synthetic caps and put them in the autoclave. Better yet, just put the open bags with a substrate in an autoclave and insert cotton caps and cords wrapped in aluminum foil.

Close the lid of the autoclave, adjust it to the desired temperature and processing time and proceed according to the instructions enclosed with the autoclave. The presence of the automatic control of the autoclave allows you to refuel and turn it on in the evening and in the morning to get packages with an autoclave-cooled substrate and sow the substrate with mycelium. When manually checking the autoclave before turning it on, make sure there is water and check its operation, focusing on the thermometer readings.

CHAPTER 4

THE SPAWN

T he term "seed" is commonly used by mushroom growers and is used to inoculate the final substrate. The purpose of the spawn is to increase the fungal biomass, previously present as a small mass of cells in a petri dish rather than a liquid culture, and to expand this mass to possibly several kilograms of fungi.

The seed is generally made up of cereal grains such as barley, wheat, rye, oats, rice, etc., colonized by the fungus. Each colonized grain, mixed in the final substrate, becomes a point where the fungus will develop, completely colonizing the bag or container containing the substrate in a few days.

To sterilize the cereals, we have to eliminate a large number of possible contaminations. Immediately after the grains are hydrated, these microorganisms begin to proliferate very quickly. Of all the microorganisms present in the grains, bacteria are the fastest growing. Bacteria can multiply every 20 minutes at room temperature on average. At such a rate, a single bacterium can multiply into more than a million cells in a matter of hours.

If only a small part of these contaminating microorganisms

survive the sterilization process, the result can be devastating, making the "seed" unusable and a vector of contamination for the other lots present as well.

Once sterilized, it is assumed that the grain of the cereal used is completely free of microorganisms. Even the air is full of suspended microorganisms and spores, the use of HEPA filters allows you to drastically reduce their presence.

Therefore, after sterilization, the containers or pouches containing the final substrate must be moved to a clean place or must remain in the pressure cooker / autoclave until they are used.

The amount of water added to the grains is another important factor. Excess water promotes the growth of bacteria, as well as slowing the growth rate of the fungus mycelium. When the hydration of the grains exceeds the threshold, they usually burst, exposing the kernel of the grain. This also promotes the development of bacteria.

The beans are immersed in boiling water in a pot for a certain time until reaching the correct point of hydration, then drained. After cooling and drying outside, the beans are placed in glass jars, containers or polypropylene bags, usually with acrylic or cotton filters.

Growers should adjust the moisture content and sterilization time based on tests and observations. A very important factor when creating your own spawn is the container air filter. During the colonization of the grains the mycelium needs to breathe, for this it is necessary to have an air filter that prevents the entry of contaminants, but at the same time releases the carbon dioxide produced by the mycelium.

Some growers use a double layer of micro-porous tape as a filter, rather than cotton wool or coffee filters. You can also find heat-resistant plastic bags made specifically for growing mushrooms with a filter built into the plastic; this allows an adequate exchange of air during the development of the mycelium.

A simple method to make a container suitable for growing the "seed" is to use glass jars such as those for jams. The lid is pierced and the filter affixed under the cap. There is also the possibility of making an entrance where the needle will inject the liquid culture, in order to minimize the chances of contamination. Just make a hole with a nail in the lid of the jar and apply a drop of thermal silicone that resists high temperatures during sterilization. This silicone needle entry port closes automatically immediately after the needle is removed.

After preparing the substrate and containers, we can fill the jars. Also, if we use jars rather than bags, we must cover the lid with a double piece of aluminum foil so that the water that condenses inside the pressure cooker when we sterilize them, does not enter the jars through the filter holes.

The next step is sterilization. Up to this point the material used did not require any kind of cleaning or treatment. We just prepared the jars, put in a filter, hydrated the cereal grains and filled the containers.

The jars or bags can be sterilized in a pressure cooker or in an autoclave. As for sterilization, the timing varies according to the volume of the material to be sterilized. Small volume containers of beans should be sterilized in a pressure cooker for 45-90 minutes. Envelopes of greater volume require longer times even beyond 2-3 hours.

After sterilization and cooling we can introduce the mycelium by adding pieces of already colonized soil or through a liquid culture. To inoculate the vessels with the liquid culture it is necessary that the inoculation takes place in a place free of contamination.

Usually in a laboratory, this procedure is performed in a laminar flow hood, where the air is filtered with HEPA filters, or inside a glove box. The glovebox consists of a transparent plastic container with 2 holes through which to put your hands in the gloves to handle the sterile objects.

There are different models and ways to build a glovebox, with a simple search on your search engine you will be able to understand which model is best suited to your needs.

Whenever the glovebox is used, it is essential to sterilize it with alcohol or an ammonia solution. Any procedure can be performed using a glovebox, from mushroom cloning, inoculating "seeds", inoculating substrates, handling culture media, Petri dishes and much more.

All materials and surfaces must be as clean as possible, but what really makes the difference is the air currents, therefore the technique. Even if you sterilize your glovebox thoroughly, there must be no drafts carrying microorganisms. So after having moved and cleaned it, it is always better to wait at least 30 minutes so that any particles left inside it fall to the base, before starting the operations.

We advise you use a sort of raised grid for all the objects, keeping them suspended above the bottom of your glovebox. By following these suggestions and moving quickly with precision, you will be able to use the glovebox avoiding contamination or at least reducing it to an acceptable percentage.

Production of "seed" using colonized grains

Once you already have a jar of 100% colonized substrate, you can use it to inoculate other jars with the freshly sterilized cereal. This technique is called "grain to grain", and is an excellent resource for rapidly multiplying the amount of "seed" exponentially.

The initial colony that was inoculated directly with a liquid culture or colonized piece of culture medium is called the primary matrix. The primary matrix, in a jar, can therefore be sorted and used to colonize another 10 cans. These 10 jars can be used to colonize another 100 and the process can go on indefinitely, contamination permitting.

Incubation of the "spawn"

After inoculation, the "seed" must be incubated. Incubation is a very important process in mushroom cultivation and essentially consists of providing the ideal conditions for the mycelium to colonize the substrate in which it is found. Light and humidity are not that important at this stage, as the containers are sealed and keep the moisture inside them. The temperature, on the other hand, must remain constant between 20 and 25°C.

During the incubation it is recommended to check the jars regularly, avoiding shaking them in order not to break the hyphae that are growing. This daily check allows you to monitor the development of the mycelium and the possible appearance of contamination. At the slightest sign of contamination you will need to discard the contents.

Some molds and bacteria can be harmful to our health as well as the mycelium, so be careful if you need to handle and eliminate them. The most common contaminations in this phase are caused by penicillium and aspergillus molds, and bacteria that make the grain rotten and slimy. Any material that smells rancid should be discarded. Usually in case of contamination the smell is pungent and will leave no doubt.

However, the mycelium has a whitish color, any other color (green, blue, orange and black spots) is indicative of contamination and must sound an alarm.

Incubation of the "seeds"

The incubator can be made in different ways, in cardboard boxes, polystyrene, switched off refrigerators or entire rooms. The temperature inside the incubator must be kept constant; incandescent lamps, aquarium heaters (for small incubators) and room heaters (in case the room is larger) can be used.

Know that incubators made with closed containers must be opened daily to renew the air. The jars have filters so that the excess CO_2 produced by the mushroom escapes. If the CO_2 escaping from the cans is concentrated inside the incubator, there will be no air exchange.

Conservation of the "seed"

Once colonized, the "seed" has a period of time before a decline in vitality occurs. As the "seed" ages, the nutrients contained in the grains are depleted, slowing the growth rate of the fungus, thus losing its vitality. The mycelium also has less ability to defend itself from any contamination.

A "seed" stays in optimal conditions for 30 days, after which it will rapidly begin to lose its vitality. However, if you don't intend to use it soon, you can keep it in the refrigerator. The "seed" can be refrigerated for a few months at a temperature never lower than 4°C (this also depends specifically on the species we cultivate). This step will slow down its metabolism and growth, extending its conservation.

CHAPTER 5
SUBSTRATES

❧⟪◯◉⟫❧

The substrate for mushrooms is a particular preparation that is found inside the bales of mushrooms to allow their cultivation at home.

People's awareness of wholesome foods has grown. In fact, many people are giving greater attention to the consumption of healthier foods and at the same time those rich in substances and nutrients that are very important for our health.

The cultivation of some species of mushrooms at home allows us to control day by day the growth of this little-used food, however precious for our body.

In the cultivation of mushrooms at an amateur level, no special tools or spaces are needed: a cellar, a garage, a garden or even just a terrace is enough to try your hand at this activity.

The satisfaction that will be obtained will be great and will also be rewarded by the benefits of eating mushrooms.

The supply of mineral elements and a natural diet with a higher intake of vegetables help us to live better.

Mushrooms grown with the inoculated substrate allow us to have controlled food, therefore it is certainly healthy.

Here are some important properties that mushrooms have: they contain very few sugars and fats for which they are indicated in diets; they are rich in minerals such as phosphorus, magnesium, potassium, selenium, copper, calcium and other antioxidant substances that stimulate and strengthen the immune system; they fight free radicals and therefore slow down the aging of skin and bones; they contain numerous vitamins, including vitamins of group B, group C, vitamin D and others; they contain amino acids and proteins, so they are also useful in vegetarian and vegan diets; they are generally cholesterol-free.

These are just some of the basic properties of mushrooms grown with the mushroom substrate, others are more specific depending on the species chosen.

Today, however, with new research and experimentation, it is possible to cultivate various species: a terrace, a cellar or a garden is enough and, at an amateur level, we can have the satisfaction of cultivating and harvesting a natural, safe, healthy and genuine product.

We can have all this comfortably at home, growing some species with the substrate for mushrooms and checking their development step by step .

Pasteurization occurs when the substrate is heated to temperatures between 65 and 85°C for a couple of hours using a hot water or steam bath. This won't kill all the harmful microbes in it, but it will give your mushrooms a good edge. Indeed, it can sometimes be beneficial if some microorganisms remain in the substrate.

STERILIZATION

To sterilize the substrate it is necessary to heat it to a very high temperature (even over 120°C) under pressure. This will eliminate all living microorganisms that would otherwise compete with your mushrooms or could even ruin them.

WHEN TO PASTEURIZE OR STERILIZE

The need to pasteurize or sterilize depends on the type of substrate being used. Those with lower nutrient levels, such as straw with no added nutrients, can be prepared using pasteurization only.

Conversely, substrates that contain very high amounts of nutrients, such as hardwood sawdust with added nutrients, must be sterilized as they are often contaminated with mold and other types of harmful microorganisms.

COMMON SUBSTRATES FOR MUSHROOMS

A good substrate shouldn't just contain all the various organic nutrients your mushrooms need to grow. It should also be easy to work with and shouldn't be too costly. Know that there is no "best" choice suitable for all types of mushrooms. For this reason, some growers like to experiment with different substrates to see which substrate produces the best results for each type of mushroom.

COCONUT FIBERS AND VERMICULITE

A blend of coir and vermiculite makes an excellent substrate for mushrooms. Coir is made from coconut shells, while vermiculite is a heat-treated foamed mineral that can hold a lot of water. A typical blend of coconut and vermiculite has a 1:1 ratio.

A mix of coconut and vermiculite isn't particularly nutritious for plants, but it's nutritious enough to grow many types of mushrooms. However, you should pasteurize it before introducing the spores.

COFFEE GROUNDS

Good gardeners know that coffee grounds can be reused. They are rich in nitrogen, so they make an excellent soil improver. Coffee grounds are also good as a substrate for mushrooms, although we don't recommend them as a first choice. The reason is that coffee grounds are very rich in organic compounds, so they can easily contaminate the crop. For this reason, it is often better to add them to other substrates such as coconut or sawdust rather than using them alone. Sterilization is ideal, but pasteurization can work too.

LOGS

Mushrooms like to eat decaying organic matter, and one such matter is dead wood. In theory, it may seem like a good idea to take a log and grow mushrooms on it, but in practice this can be expensive. First, not all mushrooms will grow on a log, as some only eat some timbers and not others. It can take a long time for the first shoots to emerge, ranging from several months to a year. On the other hand, it can be worth it if you're only doing it for decorative purposes in your garden. Once inoculated, a trunk can produce mushroom shoots for many years and requires no maintenance or sterilization!

LIVE TREES

Fungi often form a beneficial relationship with other organisms called a mycorrhizal association. In our case, the other organisms would be trees. If you walk outdoors, you may come across trees with fungi that naturally grow along their trunk or branches. For our purposes, it would not be easy or very practical to inoculate a real tree with mushroom spores, although it might be possible. For growing mushrooms at home it is better to use logs.

MANURE

Many species of mushrooms love nothing but manure.

SOYBEAN SHELLS

Soybean shells make another good substrate for growing mushrooms. You can get great results by mixing them with hardwood sawdust. Depending on the type of mushrooms you are growing, it may take a little experimentation to find the optimal ratio. You can start with a 1:1 ratio and work from there.

MIXTURES OF WOOD FLAKES OR SAWDUST

Along with coir and vermiculite blends, wood sawdust is another commonly used substrate for mushroom growing. What makes it attractive, among other things, is that it is a waste product of the wood industry, which means that it is widely available and cheap. However, sawdust is rarely used alone, but is typically mixed with wood chips to improve its structure and colonization rate. Not all types of sawdust work well for mushrooms - it must come from hardwood such as oak or maple.

As an alternative to hardwood sawdust, you can use wood pellets. These products are readily available because they are used for wood stoves. Before inoculating, the pellets must be immersed in water and broken down into sawdust.

STRAW

Straw is an excellent substrate for growing mushrooms. As a waste product from agriculture, it is usually very cheap, so you can get a lot of it for very little money. While your mushrooms will love straw, be aware that it can be a bit messy to work with because you have to cut, clean and pasteurize it. Unless you're a commercial mushroom grower who buys huge quantities of straw from a farm, it's probably worth buying a small pack at a garden store. This straw is often already cut and cleaned. To pasteurize it, throw the straw into a container and sprinkle it with hot water.

The solution? Purchase the bales with mushroom substrate

On the market, there are special kits, if you want to try your hand at this type of cultivation. They are real packages that, in different forms, contain the substrate already "inseminated" with the spores and the mycelium.

Of course, each species of mushroom needs a suitable substrate to recreate as much as possible the natural environment in which it grows, even if the treatments to promote fruiting are similar for all, with particular attention to the temperature compared to the cultivation period.

These are the cultivable mushroom species that need little care and that ensure a more than satisfactory success.

The substrate for Champignon Mushrooms

It is one of the most common mushrooms used for growing at home. The best substrate for this mushroom species consists mainly of straw of different types and other organic material suitable for sowing the spores.

This particular type of substrate can be found packed in mushroom bales. These products can be purchased in specialized farms even if, compared to pleurotus bales, for example, it is quite difficult to find.

CHAPTER 6
PASTEURIZATION OF STRAW

S traw is a main ingredient for preparing the substrate, which constitutes one of the fundamental raw materials for any grower. Its use is essential in the preparation of the substrate for Cardoncello, Pleurotus ostreatus and other related species. The Pleurotus ostreatus is the fastest and easiest species to grow, and is the one I recommend you start with.

What is described in this chapter is one of the many methods for pasteurizing straw in a do-it-yourself way, in our opinion the simplest, fastest and most home-friendly. Obviously, it is a quick and easy little guide, if you have more straw to sterilize you can then equip yourself with pots, and then boil directly. The most used types of straw are that of wheat and that of rice, but those of other cereals could also be fine, but we recommend straw of good quality, of wheat (no hay): if you wonder if simple hay is fine, the answer is NO.

It is true that its composition is not very different from straw, however, it contains many more seeds, which would multiply the risks of contamination, being particularly appetizing for bacteria.

If you want to try hay, taking care to manually eliminate all the seeds you see, you can do it, but the result is a little less certain.

Preparation of Straw substrate, 1st Phase

First, we take a plastic bucket, together with a sufficiently large cloth bag (even an old pillow case is just fine), and thus cut the straw into small pieces, put it in the bag, and place the bag in the bucket.

Cutting it manually with scissors is a rather tedious operation, if you want to work with some other system, go ahead. To prepare a 5 kg block you need about 2 / 2.5 kg of dry straw, which we must hydrate.

Preparation, 2nd Phase

We close the bag, and boil a quantity of water sufficient to completely submerge the straw. You can also use more pots. In this case we used 4 medium-large pots.

When the water boils, we remove it from the stove and pour it onto the bag, being careful not to burn ourselves!

We put a lid or a plate on the bag that we have just poured boiling water onto, to keep it completely submerged in water, and put a weight on it so that it stays at the bottom.

Preparation, 3rd Phase

Having done this, we now have to keep the bag submerged for about 2 hours, taking care not to let it cool quickly. We can wrap the bucket in a blanket or a sleeping bag, so as to prevent it from cooling too quickly.

Now we just have to remove the bag and hang it in a suitable place to drain, for at least 3 to 4 hours, to eliminate excess water.

At this point the pasteurization is over, now we just have to inoculate our straw, so we will need a transparent bag large enough to contain the contents of the original bag. For small quantities, freezer bags of 1 to 2 liters are also good.

However, take care to use new bags and not shopping bags, because even if it is true that a sterile environment is not necessary, we must still use a minimum of caution.

4th Phase - The Fresh mycelium

So let's take our jar of mycelium.

Now start filling the bag with straw, at each layer of straw, alternate with a handful of mycelium dosing it so that it is enough to completely fill the bag.

As we fill the bag, we will have to press each layer down well with our hands, in order to eliminate excess air. Once filled, we crush the bag; leaning on it works well

We will have to apply a filter (a padded seat cover is also fine) clean well and sterilize with alcohol, so as to allow the mycelium to "breathe" during colonization, and prevent any contaminants from being able to ruin our work.

We have reached the final point, and at this point our dance is ready. If we have done everything correctly, we will see the mycelium reborn and clone day by day.

5th Phase - Incubation

Now we just have to place our bags in a dark place, and maintain a temperature of between 22° and 25°, until complete cloning of the mycelium, i.e. when the substrate is completely white.

After about 1 month the mycelium should have completely invaded the straw, and if so, the compound can be taken to a dimly lit place out of direct sun and wind, at a temperature between 15 and 20°C (depending on the variety).

Make some cuts / holes or remove the upper part of the bag and start spraying the substrate with water 2/3 times a day, to give birth to the first mushrooms after a few weeks.

Last Phase - Good harvest and good tasting

Now you just have to observe, wait and collect your tasty ripe mushrooms, fresh and fragrant.

CHAPTER 7

GROWING MUSHROOMS: NOTIONS OF STERILIZATION

꿈ᘏᗝᓂ꿈

I n this chapter we will go into the part that is considered by many to be the most delicate in the mushroom cultivation process. Any lack of attention during this step can lead to contamination making all our efforts in vain.

The first step in mushroom cultivation, taking into account that you want to go through all stages of their production, is to learn how to work with the culture medium, with sterilization methods and good laboratory practices so that there is no contamination in any stage of the process.

The culture medium is a kind of jelly containing nutrients and other substances in its formula that provide the necessary conditions for the growth of the mycelium. This gelatin is composed of nutrients, necessary for the growth of numerous microorganisms, and agar, which is the powder extracted from algae responsible for the gelatinous consistency of the culture medium.

Different microorganisms have different nutritional needs, so the culture medium is created according to the needs of the specific microorganism to be grown.

There are different types and applications of culture media in microbiology, but in mushroom cultivation we are only interested in those formulated to optimize mycelium growths that produce fungi. The culture medium suitable for the growth of the mycelium of the fungus you are growing also allows the growth of other microorganisms, such as bacteria, molds and yeasts.

STERILE ENVIRONMENT TO PREVENT CONTAMINATION

We can say with certainty that we live surrounded by microorganisms. In the air itself there are a multitude of spores, bacteria and organisms invisible to the naked eye. Every part of our body is inhabited by an infinite number of microorganisms of all kinds. Our house, every object, our clothes, practically everything around us is full of fungi, bacteria and spores.

This makes creating a sterile work environment no easy task. Therefore, to work with the culture medium, during all the processes involved in the cultivation of mushrooms, it is necessary to have some knowledge about sterilization techniques and laboratory work.

Knowing the techniques does not necessarily mean that you need a laboratory to be able to grow mushrooms. There are several ways that allow you to do this job even at home, on a small and medium scale, which we are going to see together.

STERILIZATION

Sterilization is the total elimination of microbiological life on any material. It is something other than just cleaning. A scalpel can be washed, be cleaned, but to be sterilized it needs to be subjected to a certain temperature and pressure for a certain period of time. This step alone will eliminate all bacteria, fungi, spores and viruses present on it.

Autoclaving is performed using an autoclave. An autoclave is like a giant pressure cooker, which boils water and creates steam under pressure. In mushroom cultivation the autoclave is used to sterilize both the culture medium, substrate blocks and any other material that needs to be sterile. To completely eliminate microorganisms from a material, it must be exposed to a temperature of 121°C, at a pressure of 15 PSI for at least 15 minutes. However, the time required varies according to the volume and density of the material to be sterilized.

A pressure cooker can perform the same function as an autoclave.

We know that at sea level the atmospheric pressure is 1 atm and water boils at exactly 100°C. This temperature is not sufficient to eliminate many naturally occurring microorganisms. However, when we apply pressure to the container, the water it contains boils at a higher temperature.

A pressure cooker works by preventing steam from fully escaping through a valve containing a weight. This weight covers the hole through which the steam escapes, and only when the internal pressure is greater than the weight of the valve is it released.

This maintains a constant pressure inside the pot.

This means that inside a pressure cooker, for example, where the internal pressure is higher than atmospheric pressure, the water can reach higher temperatures before boiling, making the steam produced hotter than 100°C. There is therefore a relationship between volume, pressure and temperature.

It is important to keep in mind that there is a relationship between altitude and the boiling point of water. For example, at sea level water boils at 100°C, but at an altitude of 5,000 meters above sea level, 94°C is enough.

Most pressure cookers do not reach the 15 PSI that autoclaves reach, but even so it is possible to sterilize materials simply by increasing their heat exposure time.

In a pressure cooker, I recommend sterilizing the jars with culture media, water and liquids in general for between 30 and 45 minutes. Although the 15 PSI required for the steam to reach 121°C is not reached, sterilization can be achieved within this time.

USE A PRESSURE COOKER TO STERILIZE

It is very common for people to ruin a pressure cooker because they are not sure how to use it. You may have already heard of a pressure cooker that has exploded.

Working with pressurized materials can be dangerous if you do not pay due attention and comply with the specifications of the pot you use.

To use the pressure cooker we must keep in mind that the water inside it can never evaporate completely during the process. You will then need to add enough water for the desired sterilization time.

Usually I put a perforated pan on the bottom of the pot, that raises the level where I place the materials and jars to be sterilized. Then I fill with 4 fingers of water. Another thing to absolutely avoid is blocking the steam outlet.

Pressure cookers are designed so that enough steam is released to maintain adequate working pressure. If the steam outlet is blocked for any reason, the pressure will continue to rise. Most modern cookware has safety devices, and if the pressure rises above a certain level, these devices release excess steam and prevent an accident. If these devices are also blocked, the pot can explode.

It is essential to put enough water in the pot and make sure that the valve is not blocked by arranging the objects internally in a suitable way.

Here are some tips for using the pressure cooker correctly:

The rubber that seals the lid dries out over time and must be replaced as often as necessary. In some pots the lid seals metal to metal directly.

Make sure the stove used to heat the pot can hold its weight.

Use the right amount of water for the desired sterilization time. You can make tests if you are not practical. Just fill the pot halfway with water and measure the amount before putting it in. Turn on the heat and allow 1 hour from when the steam starts to escape. Then turn off the stove waiting for the steam to completely escape, and measure the amount of water left. This way you will know how much water evaporates per hour, and you can use it as a reference.

When the pot reaches pressure, it pushes the weight of the valve upwards causing the steam to escape, the flame should be adjusted to keep a steady stream of steam from escaping.

At the end of the sterilization process, turn off the heat and place the pot in a suitable place to cool down overnight. If you are sterilizing the culture medium, the material must be removed while it is still warm, otherwise it is best to wait for the material to reach room temperature.

What to sterilize in the pressure cooker to grow mushrooms?

To grow mushrooms, as I have already said, it will not be necessary to go through all the stages of cultivation. You can start cultivation by purchasing ready-to-use liquid or "seed" crops, without needing to sterilize anything.

But you may need to sterilize the growing medium, the grains for spawning and the final substrate containing sawdust and grains. There is another option that uses pasteurization. In the case of a straw-based final substrate, pasteurization rather than sterilization may be sufficient.

How long does it take to sterilize?

Culture media, water, liquids in general: 25 to 40 minutes.

Tins up to 1 liter volume containing cereals: 50 to 80 minutes.

Bags up to 2 kg of cereal substrate with integrated sawdust: 90 to 120 minutes.

CHAPTER 8
PASTEURIZATION OF MANURE

⁂

garicus bisporus (the most cultivated species of all) for example is grown on a substrate composed of manure and straw. First of all, it should be noted that not all types of manure can be used. Only those of herbivorous animals are suitable, for example horse, cow, goat, sheep. Even that of hens can be used successfully. Pig manure should not be used.

Before being used, the manure must undergo a composting process, in order to make it "stable". Later I will dedicate a guide to this technique.

To simplify your life, you can use the manure commonly sold in gardening shops and also in supermarkets: it is already composted, very similar to normal soil and the only necessary treatment is pasteurization.

You will need as large a pot as possible (if you have a Presto or an All American that's fine), glass jars of equal size (as many as the pot can contain without overlapping them, or less if you don't need so many) and a meat thermometer.

First put on a pair of waterproof gloves and pour the manure into a bucket or similar container.

The consistency is that of soil.

Now add water until it is completely covered, and mix well.

At this point, take a handful of manure and squeeze it firmly in your hands, until as much water as possible comes out. Once you have "squeezed" the water out, put the handful inside the first jar. Repeat the operation until it is full, and continue the operation with all the others. After the operation, rinse the sides of the jars to remove the dirt (being careful not to wet the contents, otherwise everything will have to be redone!).

Cover the jars with aluminum foil and place them inside the pot. Add water to three quarters the height of the jars.

At this point, turn on the gas without putting the lid on the pot.

The goal is to make the central part of each jar reach a temperature of 60°C. This will take approximately 20 to 30 minutes. We can monitor the temperature with a meat thermometer, which costs a few euros.

The thermometer should be inserted halfway into the central jar.

As soon as the temperature reaches 60°C, turn off the gas and put the lid on. The temperature will continue to rise to about 70 degrees, and then it will start to drop.

After an hour and a half, two at the most, remove the jars and let them cool.

Once the jars have cooled, the manure is ready to use. We can pour it into plastic containers or bags, mixing it with spawn. Within a few days it will be possible to notice the growth of the mycelium.

When all the substrate is invaded by the mycelium, it is ready to bear fruit.

You can also bury the substrate block outdoors in a suitable location; in this way you can give rise to a perennial outdoor cultivation.

By doing so, the mushrooms will be produced in the normal growing periods: autumn and spring.

CHAPTER 9

GROWING SHIITAKE MUSHROOMS ON LOGS

❧⦿❧

Many years ago, I watched a French TV program on Sundays. Each week they went on a different excursion to visit specialty food manufacturers.

Even though I only understood half of what was said, I looked forward to the next episode because the places visited by the presenter were always charming, rustic and romantic farms or haciendas. In other words, they were exactly what I dreamed of for my future home!

In one episode, the guest was in the woods with a traditional truffle hunter. The man used a dog trained to smell truffles to track down underground truffles and collect them. The dog dug up the truffles and then was rewarded with a dog treat.

In another episode, nearly the entire show was filmed in a stone basement where mushrooms were grown on large wooden trays with manure. The light would have interrupted the mushroom growth cycle. So the cameraman had to shoot the film using the paranormal lights used for ghost hunting. This made mushroom operations feel very mysterious and serious.

After seeing these programs, I developed a deep appreciation for edible mushrooms and the people who grow or research them. I also became addicted to eating mushrooms most days. That's why I started spending too much money at the farmer's market, filling my basket with all kinds of exotic mushrooms.

Home grown mushrooms

When we finally bought the house of our dreams, I thought I'd try to inoculate some hazelnuts with truffle seeds. But, I found out how expensive it was to get started and how long I'd have to wait for truffles and chose not to. So I thought about building a basement and growing mushrooms underground ...

Thankfully, before we tidied up the brickwork and got down to business, we discovered how easy it is to grow shiitake mushrooms (at least relatively)!

Unlike truffles, which take 5 to 7 years to grow, or mushrooms grown underground that need perfect darkness and shade to grow, it only takes a year of patience and partial shade to grow shiitake on tree trunks.

How to grow shiitake mushrooms on logs

We also need to inoculate the shiitake trunks. But luckily, that's easy enough! This is how it is done.

Step 1: Order your seeds

To grow shiitake mushrooms, you need to lay eggs. The seeds

are basically like shiitake seeds that you will plant in your trunks. You can buy them in specialized stores.

Spawning occurs in two forms: thorns and sawdust. To use sawdust, you need to purchase a special syringe called an "inoculation tool". This tool sucks up the sawdust seeds and injects them into the logs. A quality inoculation tool can be expensive to purchase. Unless you're sure you want to do this often, I suggest you start with pegs.

The pegs are wooden dowels that are inserted into pre- drilled holes in the logs. When you buy them, they already have the seed inside of them.

Sawdust seeds and candle seeds fall into three different categories: potent (also called 'WR'), cold and hot. These categories refer to the temperatures at which the logs can 'bear fruit'. Fruiting is the term used when the logs produce shiitake mushrooms. The wide range is probably the easiest for beginners to use.

Some suppliers have what they call "proprietary varieties" of shiitake. Others offer many different varieties.

For starters, I recommend placing your order from a supplier whose climate is similar to yours. Or, choose the variety that the vendor finds easiest to grow.

Seeds must be refrigerated (not frozen) on arrival until ready for use. Also, for best results you want to use them one or two months after receiving them.

Step 2: Get your logs

Then you will need to get some hardwood logs. When buying your seeds, the seller should offer you the best types of wood for the stock you are buying. For most strains, red oak is my favorite for shiitake.

Logs should not be cut more than 6-8 weeks before inoculation to reduce the risk of competing mushrooms occupying your shiitake logs. They should also be aged at least two weeks after cutting to allow the terpenes that prevent fungi from growing on healthy trees to dry out.

The logs must be cut to 36-40 cm in length to facilitate handling. They should also be around 3-8cm in diameter, so they have enough wood for the shiitake to colonize, but not be too heavy for them to be lifted. You also want your logs to have thick, intact bark, so the wood inside stays moist longer.

Step 3: Collect the tools

If you want to be professional and vaccinate hundreds of logs every year (as we do), you can invest in special equipment. An angle grinder equipped with a custom tip and an inoculation table with rollers for rotating the logs can speed things up. However, for the first time, I recommend that you start with the tools you already have to gain some experience.

Here are the tools you need to use the replacement cap:

A 5-7 cm drill bit

A piece of tape

A hammer

You just want to drill to the depth of your spawning hook. So take one of your shiitake caps and hold it to the end of the tip. Then wrap a piece of duct tape around the tip to mark the length of the cap. This piece of duct tape will be your guide, so you know when to stop drilling and don't drill too deep.

Optional:

Jar of wax

A heat source for use with the stove (e.g. camping stove, electric burner)

Wax smear

Food paraffin wax

Unless you live in an area where it rains and the humidity is high most of the time, you will get the best results by sealing the corks with wax. So even if wax sealing is not necessary, I recommend it for many places.

Step 4: A Baby Trial! Training!

Now, for the fun part, you need to drill holes for all the plugs.

I'm being ironic. Drilling is the longest stage and can be tedious. So put on some music, invite some friends over and throw a party!

For best results, a diamond pattern should be used when drilling the holes. Start a few centimeters from one end of the log and drill lengthwise holes every 4 centimeters. Stop a few inches from the other end. Note: It is not recommended to drill only at the ends of the logs as these areas tend to dry out too quickly.

Start the next row about 2 cm from the first row. Again, drill the holes about 5cm apart. Then go down the next row to the end of the log.

The number of holes to be drilled varies according to the length of the log and its diameter. However, it is recommended that you keep a rough count as you go, so that you don't make more holes than you need to fill.

Step 5: hammer in the plugs

Now you need to put a plug in each hole and hammer them in. Hammer until they are flush with the trunk. Hammering is so much fun! Don't hit your thumb. (I already did.)

Step 6 (optional): Apply the wax!

If you have chosen to use wax, now is the time to melt it and spread it a little on the holes where you hammered the plugs. Cover the entire hole, but don't worry about making it thicker. A little bit will be fine.

Phase 7: Water and wait

Store the logs in a shaded area. Under a small canopy of trees, for example at the edge of a forest, it is perfect. If you don't have this, you can use a shade cloth to create an ideal space.

Keep your logs off the floor. You can put them on a piece of wood or on a pallet. Stack them like firewood. You want to maintain good air circulation around the logs.

Keep your logs moist all the time. Like in a garden, if it rains an inch and there isn't much dry wind, that should be enough. But when it's not raining, take out the hose or watering can and wet the logs with 2 or 3 gallons of water every week until the rain returns.

Step 8: Be fruitful and celebrate

About 12 months later, you will begin to see what look like small mushrooms forming where your plugs were put in. When this happens, soak your logs in a tub of water overnight. Then stand them upright.

Well, guess what?

Yup! The Shiitake are coming! (You knew this was going to happen, right?)

In general, growing shiitake mushrooms is the easiest. It is also one of the most rewarding crops you can grow at home. Considering they cost 16 euros a pound at the farmer's market and add so much pleasure to your palate, they are worth the time and effort.

It's the perfect time to start, so go ahead and grow shiitake! Then don't hesitate to try growing oysters or leonina mushrooms on the logs as well. Go wild!

CHAPTER 10
GROWING CHAMPIGNONS AT HOME

꽃〓ⓞ〓꽃

Fungi differ from plants by having no roots, leaves or stems. They are made up of filaments of cells held together in bundles, but the fungi have no chlorophyll and do not need the sun to grow, they feed on organic matter from the outside.

Champignon mushrooms are edible and are among the most used in cooking, of which the upper part, the stem and the cap are mainly used. The part of the fungus that remains in the substrate in which it grows is called mycelium and is an intertwining of filaments that resembles the roots and constitutes the vegetative apparatus of the fungi.

Like all mushrooms, champignons also grow from spores, cells that have the same function as seeds. When they find the right conditions, they germinate and produce structures called hyphae that branch and form mycelium. Growing champignon mushrooms at home is simpler than it seems and is one of the foods that, once eaten, always grows back as long as it finds nutrients in the substrate.

What do you need to grow champignon mushrooms at home?

✓ A large styrofoam box with lid, which does not mold and does not rot, keep the temperature and humidity constant. Pretty good boxes with lids are for sale on Amazon.

✓ Compost

✓ Mulch for cover and straw.

✓ Dry (or fresh) mycelium of Agaricus Bisporus, the scientific name of champignons, which is often indicated on packages as "champignon" (which in reality would be Agaricus Campestris). It is easily found at seed dealers.

✓ Of course, water.

What to do to grow champignons at home?

Combine the straw with the compost, moistening a little with water. If it is not sterilized, it may be convenient to boil the straw first to avoid the germination of other mushrooms accidentally already contained in it. Also add some coffee grounds that help mushroom development.

This compound is the substrate in which your champignons will grow, the more there is the more nutrients the mushrooms will have. Put everything in the Styrofoam box.

Spread the dry mycelium and cover with moistened mulch, sprinkling a little water.

Close the box with the lid for about a week to prevent light from entering. Keep it moist until you see a thin white layer on the substrate, a sign that the mycelium has colonized the surface, but don't overdo it with water.

Prepare a taller lid for the box to allow the mushrooms to have enough space to grow tall. Also make a small central hole to let in some indirect light, but covered with cling film to keep humidity and heat out.

Keep the humidity in the box constant around 80%, never directly wetting the mushrooms with water.

After about twenty days, the first champignon mushrooms grown by you should be ready to harvest and eat. The mushroom cap must have a diameter between 5 and 8 centimeters, with the lower part slightly pink. Just bend them slightly and pull them to detach them from the substrate.

If the whole process for growing mushrooms at home goes well, you can also have a weekly harvest and add mushrooms to many organic dishes to prepare in the kitchen, especially salads with other crops from your garden.

4 final tips for growing champignons at home

The ideal temperature for growing mushrooms is between 22 and 27°C. In any case, avoid keeping them in an environment that is too hot because otherwise the development stops.

Use a nutritious compost, it is very important to make the mushrooms grow well with all the substances they need.

You can keep the mushroom grow box even in the garden, on the balcony or terrace, but the ideal place is a dark room such as a closet or garage.

All the humidity necessary for the growth and development of fungi is in the earth, so it should never dry out completely and use a diffuser to avoid excess watering.

CHAPTER 11
CULTIVATING ENOKIS AT HOME

❧❀❧

Like other mushrooms, enokis are sometimes used medicinally, to treat liver infections and boost immune system responses. Some believe these little mushrooms can help shrink tumors. Growing enokis at home requires careful application of heat, cold and humidity at different times throughout the growth cycle. Useful things to have:

Plastic bottles,

Soap,

Culture medium,

Enoki mycelium.

1

Clean and sterilize clear plastic bottles or cylinders, each measuring approximately 8 inches tall. Wash the bottles with antibacterial soap and rinse thoroughly with warm water to ensure no soap residue remains.

2

Mix aged wood sawdust or professional mushroom growing

medium with enoki mycelium. You can find eggs, as well as culture media, at garden centers, nurseries or mushroom-specialty dealers. This must be thoroughly mixed in the medium to promote growth.

3

Fill the plastic bottles with the breeding medium. Store the bottles in an area with temperatures ranging between 72 and 77 degrees F, and relative humidity above 90 percent. Exposure to light doesn't matter; humidity and high temperature will encourage growth.

4

Check the bottles after two weeks of growth. You should see thin strands of mycelium starting to spread throughout the bottle; this is essentially the mushroom roots. Keep the enoki mycelium in a warm and humid environment until the mycelium has completely covered the culture medium; this can take anywhere from two weeks to a month.

5

Transport the bottles to a cool place, with temperatures ranging between 50 and 65°C. Humidity can drop in this cold place. Again, sun exposure doesn't matter. The sudden change of atmosphere will cause the mycelium to produce the characteristic bodies of the fungus; these can be collected within 60 days of initial production.

CHAPTER 12

CULTIVATING THE LION'S MANE

❧❧❧❧❧❧

L ion's mane mushrooms (Hericium erinaceus) are the envy of the world of mushrooms, with their incredible waterfall and ice cube shape. In nature, it almost looks like coral has escaped from the ocean and clung to a tree. Beyond its unusual appearance, there is a delicacy, with a sweet and meaty taste of crab.

Growing lion's mane indoors has become more popular in recent years, with the emergence of strains that are constantly being improved, and for good reason. Not only do they taste delicious, but they also have valuable medicinal properties. Currently, they are being studied for their ability to prevent dementia and relieve anxiety. They have also been shown to help protect the heart and control diabetes.

While they may be a little tricky for novices to grow, they're not the hardest mushrooms to grow, and you can have your own batch of mushrooms in just a few weeks.

The lion's mane can grow on sawdust or hardwood logs. One batch will reliably produce at least three crops. You can grow lion's mane on logs or buy substrate online if you can't find them locally. Ready to get started?

Lion mushroom cultivation on logs

Growing lion's mane on logs is a surefire way to have a stable and reliable crop for years to come.

Choose a substrate

The lion's mane grows only on hardwood. The best varieties are oak, maple and birch. Maple is the preferred wood. The lion's mane is one of the few mushrooms that grows on black walnut.

Tulip, poplar and willow also lend themselves to short-term production. In the long run, choose elm, chestnut, oak, or black walnut.

The age of the wood is also important. They will not grow on wood that is too green or overgrown with other fungi.

Newly cut trees or branches or newly pruned branches are most effective. Winter pruning is ideal because that's when the tree has a high sugar content, which is beneficial for the fungi.

The logs must have a diameter of about 30 cm. It is preferable that they are also of uniform length. I find 1 meter long logs to be the easiest to handle. Keep in mind that part of the work involves moving logs when wet, and a wet log can be heavy.

Dry logs

Place the logs on a pallet or other raised surface to dry for 1 to 3 months. You want them to contain only 40% moisture.

Don't keep the logs near firewood. They can catch diseases and insects.

Once your logs have dried, you are ready to inoculate them. This can be done at any time of the year, but spring is the best time.

Now is the time to purchase the amount of breeding stock you need for the number of logs you have seasoned. For example, 100 caps can inoculate 10 logs.

Inoculation tools

Several elements are required to complete the inoculation process. You probably already have several.

Assuming you intend to inoculate 10 trunks, you will need:

A pound of sealing wax. You can use cheese quality wax or mushroom wax, but don't use ordinary candle wax, as it is not sterile.

A hammer or rubber mallet.

A small paintbrush or turkey watering can.

Cordless drill with a 5-6 cm bit equipped with a stop collar.

Double boiler.

Candy thermometer.

Inoculation of your logs

Drill each log with rows of holes. Personally, I'm not good at making holes in a straight line, so I use a chalk line. By measuring everything, I can get the most out of each log.

Melt the wax in a double boiler. Use a candy thermometer to

make sure the temperature stays below 212°F. Too hot and it will kill the seeds.

Drill holes one and a half centimeters deep and 8 cm apart in rows of 4 cm. Alternate the starting point of your holes from the top of the log.

After drilling a log, start placing the plugs. It is best to complete only one log at a time, so that the holes do not get contaminated.

Use a hammer to gently tap the replacement plugs into the holes. The plug must be flush with the surface of the wood.

Use the brush or basket to place the wax on the cap and hole.

Soak your log for 12-24 hours, but no longer.

Take care of your logs

Once inoculation is complete, your logs are ready to be stacked in a shady, humid place. They can be stacked like a crib or placed on a support at a 45° angle.

If you have trouble maintaining humidity levels in your lion mushroom culture, try partially burying the logs in an upright position.

The logs must be located in a shaded area with adequate air circulation. A patch of mature conifers is a good thing, or failing that, build a three-sided shelter. Pieces of fabric with 80% opacity are ideal for this.

Lion's mane is not a fast growing crop on logs. It can take up to

2 years for them to really bloom. Your logs will bear fruit for up to 6 years.

You can check the ends of the logs to see if there is white fluff on them, which tells you that the mycelium has grown all over the trunk and that everything is growing properly.

Lion's mane cultivation in sawdust

Lion's mane can also be grown in sacks using sawdust or wood pellets as a substrate. This is often referred to as a fruiting block. Bags are usually grown indoors.

This method is faster and more manageable, but more expensive.

The lion's mane prefers temperatures between 65 and 75° until fruiting, and it takes about 3 weeks to ripen this way.

Making a block of sawdust

Create your block of sawdust by combining:

Five cups of sawdust.

A cup of wheat bran to add nutrients.

Six cups of hot water.

A cup of molasses.

Keep adding water until the mixture is clumped, and some of the water drips off if you squeeze it.

Once done:

Put the mixture in a grow bag. Fold and seal according to the instructions.

Sterilize them in a pressurized jar. Place a wire rack or lids to cover the bottom of the can and press the bag with a plate or bowl. It is necessary to sterilize for 2.5 hours to make sure all bacteria are killed.

Inoculation of your sawdust blocks

Before starting, make sure your hands and work area are clean to avoid contamination.

Add the seed to your block of sawdust and mix well. It takes about one pound of seed for every five pounds of the mixture.

Put the bag in a dark and warm place to let it grow. It will take a few weeks for the mycelium to spread into the bag. It is natural for the block to start turning brown.

Punch holes in the plastic bag in several places. Make lots of holes to make smaller fruit, or use fewer holes to encourage larger fruit.

Place the block in the growing area, which should have indirect light and some air movement.

Take care of your sawdust blocks.

Now that your colony is established, it will start making pins, which should start forming within a week or two.

Check your blocks once a week. Look for any mold, other fungus, or dry areas. The lion's mane thrives best in a humid environment, so be sure to keep it moist.

Problems and solutions for the cultivation of lion's mane

Mold

Logs and blocks can develop mold. If they do, move them around so they have better air circulation. If they are too infested, throw them away.

Drainage

The opposite of the mold problem: growing lion's mane on logs and blocks can dry out. Try moving the logs to a better place or soaking them.

If you find that your blocks dry out too quickly, you can place them in an empty bucket or aquarium to help retain water. You can also spray them with water using a nebulizer.

Collection and storage

Once the lion's mane has formed, it needs to be harvested before it turns pink or brown. Look for when the light colored teeth have formed, usually 4 to 7 days after braces appear.

Cut the ball near the base, being careful not to damage the spine.

Place them in the refrigerator immediately after harvest in a ventilated container. They can be stored in the refrigerator for up to two weeks.

The lion's mane can be used as a substitute for seafood in almost any recipe. Try slicing it and making "crab" mushroom cakes, or slicing it and frying it in butter.

Drying

If you can't eat them fresh, save the lion's mane mushrooms by drying them. Cut them into 1-4 cm thick slices and place them in a well-ventilated place until dry.

What to do with used blocks

If you are using sawdust blocks, you can add them to the compost pile when they are used up. In fact, they can rejuvenate compost and produce an extra mushroom wash or two.

Adding fertilizer to the mycelium in your garden is excellent for your vegetables. The mycelium forms a symbiotic network and extracts nutrients from the soil to make them more available to vegetables.

Whether you grow them to eat or sell them at the farmer's market - you can get 20 euros a pound - growing lion's mane is an adventure worth having.

CHAPTER 13
HOW TO GROW MUSHROOMS WITH COFFEE GROUNDS

❧✦◉✦❧

The fruits of the undergrowth: mushrooms. We will never know them all unless, among you foodies, there are expert mycologists.

We are talking about edible and special mushrooms because they were grown from coffee grounds. Of course, it may seem strange but it is very easy to transform waste into a resource and this is no secret!

Not all types of mushrooms, however, can be grown this way. Porcini mushrooms, the so-called symbiotic mushrooms, therefore linked by a relationship of exchange of substances with trees, are not included in the list.

Coffee waste is an excellent substrate for growing mushrooms because it contains minerals and nutrients that are essential for the growth of these organisms.

Procedure for growing mushrooms from coffee waste.

This method, which was invented by a Chinese mycologist, stands out for its circularity: it is ecological and economical and you can try it for zero waste at home!

Coffee grounds, thanks to the high temperatures to which they are subjected are sterilized in a natural way and therefore molds and bacteria cannot develop. In addition, they have a lot of nutrients such as phosphorus and nitrogen.

Equip yourself with:

Durable plastic bag.

Recycled wooden fruit box.

Mushroom seeds.

Keep the coffee at room temperature.

Put the bag inside the fruit crate and pour the mixture of coffee, alternating with the seeds of the mushrooms, into it. Close the bag and store it in a cool dark place for about 15-20 days. When you start to smell the mushrooms you will have to cut the bag with a small knife and expose it to direct sunlight.

You will harvest the first mushrooms after 3 weeks.

With this self-production technique we also discovered a startup that knows about mushrooms we want to talk to you about: Espresso Mushrooms! An all-Italian idea led by the Blue Economy which has created kits to produce mushrooms with zero impact on the environment.

Mushrooms, when edible, represent a nutrient-laden ingredient, which is why they have also been called the "meat of the poor".

These organisms are very useful to our immune system, so much so that they are considered a natural antibiotic.

They are also ideal for losing weight because they contain a negligible amount of fat and play an important role in the beauty of the skin. In fact, they contain selenium and antioxidants, substances useful for strengthening nails, hair and teeth.

And we could go on and on about the properties, but we'll stop at vitamins B2, B3 and D.

Despite all these properties, and even if edible, mushrooms contain a minimal dose of toxicity, so it's best to follow grandma's advice and eat them in moderation.

The reaction and absorption, in fact, vary from person to person so the real advice is not to overdo it because you could develop intolerances!

We can't say the same about coffee, so if you have more coffee left over and you have already grown your mushrooms, you can always reuse it in other ways, for example for gardening!

CHAPTER 14

SOME TECHNIQUES FOR THE
CULTIVATION OF MUSHROOMS

G athering them in the woods is beautiful, but knowing how to grow mushrooms at home, seeing them grow and enjoying them as soon as they are ready at any time of the year is an even more rewarding experience. Let's see together the simplest techniques for growing fresh mushrooms even in small domestic spaces.

Why buy them at the supermarket at often prohibitive prices when you could learn how to grow fresh mushrooms directly in your home in a simple and cheap way? The direct cultivation of mushrooms is the best alternative to harvesting in the woods (linked, moreover, to the seasonality of the product) and to purchasing them from the greengrocer. Through our suggestions you will discover how to grow fresh mushrooms and obtain generous harvests, free of chemical or phytosanitary residues.

How to grow canned mushrooms

What do we need?

1 high-edged wooden, plastic or polystyrene box.

1 substrate suitable for the growth of mycelia.

1 plastic sheet.

1 good garden compost.

30 gr of ready-made champignon mycelium.

leaves or straw.

how -to-grow-mushrooms-box.

Growing mushrooms in boxes is simple, even for the less experienced.

Preparation. The direct cultivation of mushrooms in the home generally takes place through boxes (made of wood, plastic or polystyrene). On the market you can buy ready-to-use boxes complete with guides on how to grow mushrooms, otherwise you can easily set up your mushroom farm using the common boxes for fruit and vegetables.

The substrate should be a mixture of well-seasoned manure, straw and dry seasonal residues. The soil to be mixed must be not too acidic and must be well sterilized: first pass it in the oven at 80°C and store it in a closed bag in the dark until use.

To successfully cultivate your mushrooms, the plastic sheet, possibly dark in color, must be placed on the bottom of the box so as to cover the entire interior. Use pegs to secure it, and let it protrude from the sides so that it can be folded back to cover the substrate when ready.

The manure mixture and the soil must be mixed very well and enriched with materials that give softness and porosity to the substrate, such as leaves and straw. In any case, by buying the ready-made compound, you will not need to resort to other materials.

The box should be filled up to 5cm below the top, moistened and left to rest for a couple of weeks before use. After this period, you can proceed with the burial of the mycelium by making small holes in the substrate at a depth of 3-4 cm, 10-12 cm apart. Once covered with other substrate and wetted with water, the ambient temperature must never drop below 20°C. Watering must be daily, avoiding excesses and water stagnation.

The ideal place to grow fresh mushrooms indoors is a garage, cellar, basement or an outdoor place sheltered from the sun and wind. A balcony, terrace, garden, simple window sill or even an enclosed space is fine as long as it maintains certain temperature / humidity conditions.

To obtain generous harvests, the ideal is to grow champignons with the box technique.

The only drawback of growing mushrooms at home is related to the musty smell that could generate from the substrate of the mycelium. In fact, to grow mushrooms quickly and lastingly, the perfect temperature is 25°C, in any case between 20 and 30°C.

After two or three weeks from the burial of the mycelium you will see a whitish mold appear, the most evident manifestation of the fungus that begins to grow. Cover it with a thin layer of smooth, compacted and moistened limestone earth and use the edges of the plastic sheet to cover the box.

In this phase the mushroom farm must be transferred to a decidedly colder environment (12-14°C) keeping the watering constant. After 15-20 days you will see the first mushrooms appear which will quickly become quite large and full-bodied.

How to grow mushrooms with wooden logs

Know that on the market there are ready-to-use kits (tee pee kits) that will allow you to grow mushrooms of different varieties and types in a really simple and immediate way. These are pre-inoculated strains with mycelium spores that can also be purchased online on specialized sites such as fieldforest.net where you can also find many practical tips on how to grow mushrooms all year round without ever leaving home.

In this, TAKE ADVANTAGE OF:

1 large container and a box to wet and keep the log moist.

1 plate just wider than the log.

1 spray bottle.

water without chlorine.

Preparation. Place the log in a shaded area, possibly outside, water it regularly and be patient for at least six months. During this period the mycelia will slowly develop inside the log until you see the first fruits emerge from the holes. This technique is perfect for growing shiitake mushrooms, a highly regarded variety of Japanese mushroom and the second most consumed mushroom in the world.

How to grow mushrooms with toilet paper

If you love to experiment with unique (not to say bizarre) cultivation techniques, one that is quite well known for growing mushrooms at home is the one based on the use of toilet paper rolls. In this way you can grow edible mushrooms of the oyster variety, which are particularly meaty and tasty. To do this you will need:

1 roll of toilet paper.

1 tee pee kit (or buy separately spores, plastic bags with filters and rubber bands).

1 box.

1 large, round plate.

1 sprayer.

water without chlorine.

Preparation. Fill a saucepan with water and bring to the boil. In the meantime, remove the cardboard tube from your toilet paper roll. Remove the water from the heat and immerse the roll in the water. When it is well soaked, let it drain and cool, taking care not to break it.

Oyster mushrooms grow rapidly on toilet paper rolls

When it is only warm, put the roll in the plastic bag contained in the kit and fill it with the grains containing the spores. Close with the special rubber bands and place the bag on a round plate and place it in the box. Place the box in the dark, in a fairly humid environment and within 3 weeks you will begin to see the first fruits grow.

At this point, place the bag in the refrigerator for 48 hours. Then, take the bag from the fridge and remove the roll, leaving it to rest at room temperature and in a lighted place for a few more days. Regularly moisten the roll with the sprayer. After 7-10 days the mushrooms will be ready and once removed from the roll (without using knives) just close the bag and wait for the mycelium to reappear to repeat the operation from the beginning.

CHAPTER 15
TIPS FOR GROWING OUTDOOR MUSHROOMS

T he optimal period for burying the loaves in open greenhouses is from September to April; this period can in any case fluctuate in relation to the seasonal trend and to the cultivation areas. Outdoor cultivation is done on land suitably protected from the sun with a 70-90% shading net, supported by normal arches for greenhouses about 5 meters wide. To protect from the wind, especially in spring, mats can be placed around the greenhouse, or polyethylene sheets about 1m high. During the harvesting period, to avoid excessive soaking from sudden and violent rains, it is advisable to have a plastic sheet, so that it can be spread, if necessary, over the tunnel. To bury the blocks, dig a trench 1m wide and about 15/20 cm deep, taking care that the walls are vertical and the bottom flat. The length of the trench will vary in relation to the number of blocks to be buried, considering an investment of 18/20 blocks for each linear meter of excavation. It is important that the ground level of the production flower beds, consisting of buried bags plus the covering soil, remains 5/10 cm higher than the adjacent paths.

Avoid keeping the bags exposed to the sun for a long time before burying. Remove the plastic wrap before settling the substrate blocks. Arrange the unwrapped packages side by side in an upright position, without breaking or squeezing them. If you want to obtain smaller mushrooms, you must leave a space of a few cm. between one layer and another, which must then be filled with sand or earth (sand can be used for filling the spaces between the packages, but not for covering them). Work with soil that is not excessively loamy or too chopped, to avoid the formation of a layer impermeable to air, a factor that can seriously compromise production. Fill in the empty spaces between the packages, then cover it all making sure that the cover does not exceed a thickness of 1 cm of earth and follow the course of the upper part of the blocks. It is very important that the cover thus obtained has lower parts (in correspondence with the spaces between the bags) and higher parts, this is because it allows to obtain rapid fruiting in correspondence with the cracks that are inevitably created on the covering soil thus arranged. It is advisable to choose soils that do not have large fragments of organic substance such as: roots, tubers, straw, turf; as these fragments or materials can be a major source of infection of particularly formidable molds. If the cultivation is repeated in flowerbeds covered by previous mushroom farms, it is very important that the residues of the already exhausted blocks are completely removed as they can host harmful parasites. If, on the other hand, you want to leave the remains of the previous cultivation in the ground, it is a good idea to wait at least two years before re-breeding. Avoid use for covering: loam, peat, sand, loamy soils and deep soils from excavations.

Moisten the covering ground with well or aqueduct water, using a dense and light jet for this.

This operation has the purpose of favoring the settling of the soil placed between the cracks of the blocks and may result in the resurfacing of the substrate, which must be immediately covered with the usual centimeter of earth and then moistened. Keep the soil of the beds moist, but not soaked, by distributing moderate quantities of water repeatedly, over one or more days, depending on the season (spring or autumn) and the climatic conditions of the growing moment (absence or presence of wind , sun, fog etc ...). It is important to avoid soil compaction with too frequent and abundant wetting, which can cause poor production, due to a reduction in gaseous exchanges between the compound and the external environment. In the initial phase of cultivation, it is advisable to let the covering soil dry out, so that cracks are created which will become easy emergency routes for the fungi. The optimal time for harvesting is when the mushroom cap, first folded down, flattens out and at the same time the first whitish spores begin to fall, forming a light patina on the carpophores. However, it is advisable to harvest before the mushrooms curl upwards, assuming a cup shape, and reach too light shades of color. The mushroom tufts must be collected whole by cutting them at the base, or simply tearing them by exerting a slight twist together, but always avoiding damaging the underlying substrate. Any stem residues left in the ground must be carefully removed and the collection point must be covered again with some earth. Stem residues not removed, but simply covered, rot quickly, damaging the next run. It is also advisable to remove from the cultivation area all fragments of fungi deriving from the harvesting and cleaning operations, because they are likewise, a major source of infection to the detriment of the entire crop. During production it is necessary to pay close attention to the possible appearance of molds (gen. DACTYLIUM), which, starting from the ground (from the remains of previously collected mushrooms and other organic materials such as straw, roots, etc.) then invade the carpophores, making them unmarketable.

In this regard, it is advisable to avoid placing wooden boards or straw or other similar material along the passageways. In cases of difficulty in passing, a little sand or other material not of vegetable origin can be distributed. Other parasites that can cause considerable damage are the larvae of some insects which penetrate inside the carpophores by digging a considerable number of tunnels with consequent depreciation of the product, or they remain in the basal portion of the stems, superficially affecting the substrate as well. The possible attacks of these insects must be addressed when an excessive number of their adults (very small gnats) are seen hovering over the mushrooms and on the cultivation beds. Before embarking on any type of fight, it is however advisable to consult a technician for the therapeutic indications to follow. At this stage, the disease that can create major problems in the production phase of mushrooms is a bacterium (gen. PSEUDOMONAS), which manifests itself first with the partial or total yellowing of the carpophores, then with a subsequent rotting of the same. Affected fungi, especially in an advanced stage of the disease, give off a characteristic smell of a putrid substance. The infection has an unpredictable course: sometimes the first run ends normally, while the second is affected by bacteriosis or vice versa. In some cases, however, the attack can even cause a loss of production. To date, no useful therapies are known to combat bacteriosis. However, it is important to keep in mind that the disease spreads from affected fungi to healthy ones with extreme ease, so to contain its expansion you must try to avoid the contagion brought by insects that move among the flower beds and by harvesting tools used by the operators. The production, due to small errors or neglect, can suffer significant drops, as an excessive layer of covering soil prevents good emergence, and an excess of soil wetting causes the appearance of deformed fungi.

Cultivation in air-conditioned greenhouses can allow the cultivation of Cardoncello in periods normally unfavorable to its growth. In this case the compost can be placed on the greenhouse flooring, contained in drawers or in cultivation beds covered with a little soil. Good results were also obtained by simply releasing the compound from the top of its casing and putting it into production without adding soil. However, it must be borne in mind that the attacks of various parasites in indoor cultivation are more difficult to contain. Under normal conditions the production cycle ends 60 days after planting and collection takes place in three flights, of which the first is the most consistent.

CHAPTER 16
GROWING MUSHROOMS IN A GREENHOUSE

❧⭑◦◉◦⭑☙

F ungi need little care because they have very few needs, however the use of a greenhouse and this particular type of cover allow to optimize the result. Consequently, the quality of the specimens is better and the flavor more intense. If you are creating a DIY mushroom greenhouse you need wooden or plastic strips, an upholstery stapler, a roll of transparent cellophane, some concrete or stoneware containers and some special soil for mushrooms.

How to grow mushrooms in a special greenhouse

Fungi grow in the absence of chlorophyll: precisely for this reason, unlike all herbaceous and tree plants, they do not have the characteristic green pigment. Consequently, the use of a greenhouse is extremely functional and improves the development of the specimens as it optimizes a process opposite to that of chlorophyll photosynthesis. In fact, mushrooms emit carbonic acid and absorb oxygen. To get the best results it is good to buy a special product in a specialized shop or, if you are passionate about DIY, you can opt for a do-it-yourself solution. In this case, suitable materials must be used: for example, the frame in which to insert the container pots where the mushrooms will grow must be made of PVC or wooden strips. These are non-toxic materials that do not rust like iron: in fact, this substance makes mushrooms poisonous.

How to make a mushroom greenhouse yourself

To create a greenhouse for mushrooms, it is first necessary to create the load-bearing frame that must support the cover. Generally, they are made of plastic or wooden strips, built with a height of 50 cm and a width of at least one meter. It is a structure that is large enough to accommodate a number of containers, but which is compact enough to avoid clutter. At this point, the covering is provided by transparent cellophane, making sure that the cover adheres perfectly to the frame. An upholsterer's stapler is used to anchor the roof and then the greenhouse base is built using refractory bricks. They are ideal as they are very resistant and are able to retain humidity and heat within the protected environment created. Once the various elements have been united, the design of the greenhouse can be completed by inserting the containers for growing mushrooms.

Mushroom greenhouse: How to grow mushrooms in a greenhouse at home

When you decide to grow mushrooms you must always keep in mind that they need a particular soil. In fact, it is necessary to provide the essential substances for development (for example sugars and proteins). For this reason it is advisable to use ready mixed and strengthened soils that are easily available in nurseries. At the same time drainage must be ensured, creating a substrate where the soil alternates with layers of peat tablets. The soil must be constantly moist, however the quantity of water administered is extremely low to avoid the formation of mold. Furthermore, the position of the mushroom greenhouse must be carefully decided: it must be placed away from direct sunlight, in a shaded and well-ventilated area.

CHAPTER 17

GROWING WINTER MUSHROOMS

❧✲◖◗✲☙

Winter mushrooms are one of those mushrooms, the cultivation of which is possible both at home and in open areas. One of the main difficulties lies in the reproduction of the mycelium, but if you master this technology, it will not be difficult to further cultivate the mycelium. Keep in mind that in order to breed winter honey mushrooms at home, you will need to allocate a window sill on the north side, as these mushrooms do not like an abundance of sunlight.

Winter honey agaric is an edible agaric of the flammulina family. Most often it can be found on willows, poplars, on the edge of the forest, along the banks of streams, in gardens and parks.

A common mushroom, it is found in the northern temperate zone. It grows in the countries of Western and Eastern Europe, Russia, Japan. It appears in September - November. In the southern regions it can be seen in December. Sometimes it occurs after snowfall, for which it got its name.

This fungus is a saprotroph, so grows on damaged and weakened deciduous trees or on dead stumps and trunks, and has a high nutritional value.

There are a number of pointers on how to distinguish winter mushrooms from other mushrooms. The cap of this species grows to 2-5 cm in diameter, very rarely up to 10 cm, is smooth and dense, cream or yellowish, sticky, mucous. The center is darker than the edges. Sometimes in the middle it becomes brownish. Tan or white lamella, white powder spore. The stalk is dense, elastic, 5-8 cm high, 0.5-0.8 cm thick, the upper part is clear and yellowish, and the lower part is brown or brown-black. This is a mushroom and differs from other honey mushroom species. The base of the leg is hairy and velvety. The taste is soft, the smell is mild.

Only caps are used for food. Winter mushrooms are used to prepare stews and soups.

Correct reproduction of the mycelium of winter mushrooms

Since the winter fungus can parasitize on living trees, it is only grown indoors. There are two methods: extensive and intensive. In the first method, mushrooms are grown on wood. With the intensive method, mushrooms are grown on a substrate, which is placed in a jar and placed on a windowsill.

As a substrate, use sunflower husk, wheat cakes, buckwheat husks, bran, beer pellets, ground corn cobs.

For proper propagation of the mycelium of winter mushrooms, the mixture must be prepared in different proportions according to the characteristics of the fillers. If the substrate consists of sawdust with bran, they must be mixed in a ratio of 3:1. The sawdust with the beer pellets is mixed in a ratio of 5:1. Similarly, it is necessary to mix sunflower husk and buckwheat husk with cereals. If sawdust is the basis of the substrate, you can add straw, sunflower husk, chopped cobs, buckwheat husks in a ratio of 1:1. All these mixtures get high yields. It should be noted that on some sawdust the mycelium grows very slowly and the yield is much lower. In addition, straw, ground corn kernels, sunflower husk can be used as the main substrate without adding sawdust. You also need to put 1% chalk and 1% superphosphate. The moisture content of the mixture is 60–70%. All raw materials should be free from mold and rot.

In the selection of containers, heat treatment of the substrate, there are many different ways. Each mushroom picker chooses his own, optimal for his case.

Any mixture must be wetted and left for 12-24 hours, then the substrate is sterilized. The wet substrate is tightly packed in jars or bags and placed in water. Bring to a boil and boil for 2 hours. In industrial mushroom cultivation, the substrate is completely sterilized in autoclaves. At home, this procedure resembles home canning of fruits and vegetables. Sterilization should be repeated the next day.

You can also put the substrate in small boxes. But sterilization is best done before packing in containers. The substrate must be well sealed during installation in the container

Sowing winter mushrooms

Before intensively growing winter mushrooms, the planting substrate, after heat treatment, must be cooled to 24-25°C. Then it is necessary to make mycelium granules, for which use a metal or wooden stick in the center of the can or package to make a hole the entire depth of the substrate. The mycelium therefore grows faster and uses the substrate over its entire thickness. The mycelium should be introduced into the hole in a ratio of 5-7% of the weight of the substrate. Then put the cans in a warm place.

Best for the mycelium is a temperature of 24-25°C. The mycelium grows within 15-20 days. It depends on the substrate, the capacity and the variety of the mushrooms. At this time, the cans with the substrate can be stored in a warm dark place, they do not need light. But the substrate shouldn't dry out. For this purpose, it is covered with a water-retaining and breathable material: canvas or thick paper. After the entire substrate is covered with mycelium, the banks are transferred to the light in a cooler place with a temperature of 10-15°C. But at the same time, direct sunlight shouldn't fall on them. The paper or canvas is removed. The necks of the cans are wrapped in cardboard and from time to time they are wetted with water to protect the substrate from drying out.

The embryos of the fruiting bodies appear 10-15 days after the exposure of the containers and 25-35 days after the sowing of the mycelium. They look like thin leg bundles with small caps. The crop can be harvested after 10 days. Bunches of mushrooms are cut and their remnants are carefully removed from the mycelium. Then the substrate is moistened by spraying it with water. After 2 weeks, you can harvest the next crop. For the entire period of growth, with a three-liter can, you can get up to 1.5 kg of mushrooms.

CHAPTER 18

HARVESTING

࿇࿇࿇

It's easy to grow your own mushrooms at home if you buy a complete kit or just lay eggs and then inoculate your own substrate. Things get a little more difficult if you grow your own mushrooms and seeds, which require a sterile pressure cooker or autoclave environment. No matter how you start them, the question of when to pick mushrooms will inevitably arise.

If you purchase a complete mushroom kit, the instructions will give you a time frame for harvesting your mushroom crop. This is really important, because depending on the conditions, the mushrooms may be ready to be harvested a few days before or after the indicated date. Also, size is not an indicator of when to pick. Bigger isn't always better. The general rule is to start harvesting the mushroom crop when the caps turn from convex to concave - bottom to top.

Oyster mushrooms should be harvested 3 to 5 days after seeing the first mushrooms begin to form. You're looking for the largest mushroom in the bunch to go from turning down at the edges to turning up or flattening at the edges.

Shitake mushrooms are grown on logs and are sold in kits. You can also create a shiitake garden by cutting your logs while the mushrooms are dormant and inoculating them yourself. The latter option requires patience, as the mushrooms will not be harvested for 6-12 months! If you buy pre-inoculated logs or sawdust blocks for the house, they should be inoculated immediately. Harvesting your shiitake mushrooms will take time and with proper care, shiitake logs can yield for 4 to 6 years or more.

Homemade mushroom picking

There is no great mystery in collecting your mushrooms, although there is a debate among amateur mycologists who hunt the species outdoors. The debate revolves around the question of whether to cut the fruit or twist and remove the fungus from the mycelium. In reality, there is no difference. The only relevant point for wild mushroom hunters is to collect mushrooms that are ripe to the point where they have distributed most of their spores so that the species continues to thrive.

Local producers can harvest in both directions, either by hand picking or by cutting. However, in the case of the homemade mushroom kit, it is not necessary to allow the mushrooms to drop the spores, so if you see a white 'dust' falling to the surface below the colony, collect it. The white "powder" is made up of spores, which means that the fruit is ripe.

CHAPTER 19

PLEUROTUS OSTREATUS MUSHROOM

BALES TO GROW AT HOME

⁘⁙⁘

Bales of mushrooms are nothing but bales of wheat straw inseminated with mycelium, in this case the Pleurotus variety ostreatus, but there are also other varieties, such as: cornucopia, champignon, pioppini, etc.

Bales offer excellent mushrooms over time but a minimum consistency of care is required. The bales should be stored in a humid and dimly lit place. In the countryside there is no problem finding a suitable place, but even on the balconies of apartments, with a little imagination, you can create a corner in which to grow your mushrooms for a long time.

Upon arrival, the bale of Pleurotus must have a white mold (even partially. This is the mycelium spores that are inoculating the bale and in doing so, create the ideal habitat for the development of the fungus.

POSITIONING: The correct position in which to hold the bale is vertical. Make small cuts of about 3-4 centimeters (ten is enough) on each side to allow the mushrooms to take air and be produced. It is important that the bales remain well covered and are sprayed at least once a day.

Ideal places for cultivation with humidity are: cellars, garages, sheds, even outdoors, making sure that the bale is sheltered from wind and rain. Not recommended places are in the house, especially if heated: dry air does not proliferate, but regresses the fungi. The birth period is estimated, that is not programmable: sometimes there are bales that produce immediately (probably because they have been sown for some time), other times it is necessary to wait longer because the sowing is recent. The ideal temperatures are from 15° to 25°C.

HOW TO COLLECT: harvesting takes place by twisting the mushroom and not cutting it, to then allow the bale to produce mushrooms again.

DURATION OF THE BALE: usually the best time to produce mushrooms at home is from September to November / December. Taking into account that the cold does not help but slows down production, we need to look for a suitable place, such as a basement, but with humidity and temperatures that do not fall below 15°C. The duration of production ranges from 3-4 months up to 6 months. Obviously, the largest collection of mushrooms takes place in the first 2 months then production will decrease.

HOW MUCH DOES A BALE PRODUCE: a bale of Pleurotus produces about half its weight, i.e. if the bale weighs 4 kg, the production will be about 2-3 kg of mushrooms while for the 8-9 kg bale the production will be 4 -5 kg. The production estimate is made based on the first 3 months.

It is necessary to respect some parameters to cultivate it in an optimal way.

So remember:

Optimal cultivation period: Autumn, early Winter and Spring, obviously it can be grown all year round.

Temperature: 15 -20°C.

Relative air humidity: 90% - relative humidity of the substrate 65/75%.

Spray the compounds 2/3 times a day in the case of dry environments, and once a day in humid environments.

Compounds should never be exposed to direct sun and wind.

However, half-light during the day and not total darkness is essential.

The mushroom reaches maturity 8/10 days after the appearance of the first carpophores (small mushrooms) and it is necessary to increase the humidity of the air up to about 90%.To avoid an excessive lowering of the temperature this operation can be carried out by putting a wet sack over the bale and proceeding with spraying of nebulized water.

It is clear that humid environments are ideal. For production it is necessary to keep the bales away from the sun and the wind, daylight is essential, so do not store in dark rooms.

If many bales are grown in the same room, it is advisable to make many air changes during production. After fruiting has begun, remember to always keep the humidity level high, the mushrooms will come out of the holes already appropriately prepared, it is not advisable to make other holes.

When the mushrooms begin to grow, it is advisable to wet them from time to time with the nebulizer. You can pick them as soon as the cap gets bigger and the previously curved edge will tend to straighten. The mushrooms must be picked with a slight rotation and not cut at the base, in order to have another reproduction, to leave the hole free until the straw is seen again.

Production:

The production of mushrooms will last about 15-20 days then do nothing, leave the mixture to rest. Do not water until you see the mushrooms reappear again for a later time, and repeat as you did for the previous run. There can be from two to four runs in all, depending on the care with which the bales were treated.

During production, the mushrooms can produce spores that you can see in the form of white powder, do not be alarmed, it is an indicator that the mushrooms have reached the maximum of their maturity and therefore must be collected and consumed.

The climate:

It influences and is fundamental for the cultivation of Pleurotus

Ostreatus, even if it is called chilblains due to its characteristic of fruiting even in winter, with temperatures between 4 and 20°C.

Too hot sun or too strong wind can prevent fruiting in part or completely.

Drought is a lethal enemy, for which the degree of humidity in the growing environment plays a decisive role.

Ambient humidity should be similar to that of autumn days after rains, in the order of about 80/90% with temperatures between 15 and 20°C.

The need to change the air satisfies two important conditions:

Remove the carbon dioxide produced by mushrooms, and lower temperatures where necessary.

This operation is a little more complicated in winter, because of the presence of cold temperatures outside.

In this case the air exchange must be reduced and partially replaced with internal air recirculation.

Change the air at least 3 times every hour.

Hygiene:

In the cultivation of mushrooms, prevention is essential.

Before storing the compound it is necessary to disinfect the premises with products based on quaternary ammonium salts, taking care to have removed any possible organic residue.

These products have a bacterial and sporicidal action at the same time.

It is a good idea to use a larvicidal insecticide as a preventative measure, especially on the walls and ceilings of the premises to prevent possible infestations of midges.

It is essential that the cultivation rooms are easily washable, with smooth, non-porous surfaces.

The floor must be as compact as possible and not give rise to water stagnation, preferably covered with a layer of concrete or alternatively with a mulching, filtering, non-slip sheet.

In some cases, hydrated lime is spread on the ground, when there is no concrete or protective sheet.

The room must have a water tap, to carry out the daily watering, it must be located in a protected manner from the prevailing winds, especially if coming from the northern quadrants.

THE CULTIVATION OF MUSHROOMS IS MORE THAN A JOB, IT'S PURE PASSION!

CHAPTER 20
PROBLEMS

❧❧❀❀

ushroom mold is the most common disease that mushroom growers encounter when breeding champignons and oyster mushrooms. Unfortunately, there are no effective ways to combat fresh mushroom mold, and crop protection is mostly timely implementation of preventive measures. The main types of mushroom molds are green, yellow, yellow-green, confetti, carmine, cobweb, and olive. Let's see what to do to prevent mold on fungi during cultivation.

Green mold. As a rule, it affects mushrooms grown in large rooms. The reason green mold appears on mushrooms is different types of skeletons, they are quite widespread in nature and appear in the substrate along with the starting materials. In addition, together with other microorganisms, they participate in fermentation. This pathogen does not suffer from high temperatures. In this case, the remaining microorganisms die, the adana fungus begins to develop even faster, without encountering obstacles and competitors. The mycelium of this fungus is composed of thin hyphae that permeate the entire substrate and give it the smell of a damp cellar. The mushroom mycelium is unable to develop under such conditions, as it does not find nutrients. It dies very quickly. And the parasitic fungus develops spores. As a result, light green, olive green and black buds appear on the substrate. The spore-bearing fungus is full of green spores. In addition, the ammonia in the substrate and the lack of fresh air only stimulate the development of this fungus. If chicken droppings are mixed unevenly into the starting mixture, this also sometimes causes green mold to appear.

Green mold can be prevented, because the starting material for substrates should only be taken in the appropriate dosage and composted correctly. The pasteurization process itself must be constantly monitored, in no case allowing overheating.

It is allowed to re-shake the substrate affected by the disease. As a result, a low yield can be achieved. Before such manipulation, the substrate is usually sprinkled with superphosphate powder.

Brown and yellow mold on oyster mushrooms and champignons

Brown mold often affects oyster mushrooms and champignons. Its causative agent is moldy saprophytic fungus. Mold can appear on the substrate before or after filling the lining material. First, the mold is white and fluffy, then it turns brown-gray, in the form of a plaque. If you pat it on your hand or pour it, the dust will lift. When the champignon mycelium sprouts into the integumentary material, the mold of the fungus disappears.

This disease can only be prevented, as treatment methods do not exist.

Yellow mold often affects champignons as well. It is caused by a parasitic fungus of the mold Myceliophtora lutea; this pathogen is one of the most dangerous for champignons. Such a mushroom can be found in nature: as a parasite on the wild mycelium of various mushrooms. And in the substrate it develops only if there is also champignon mycelium. A whitish mycelium appears at the boundary between the coating material and the substrate. After that the spores form and the affected areas turn yellow. The substrate itself begins to smell like copper oxide or carbide. The spores of the fungus are quite resistant to high temperatures, do not die during pasteurization and can be transported with the infected soil from the substrate through the hands of people and tools.

For preventative purposes, it is necessary to strictly comply with sanitary requirements, and the appropriate compost. If the substrate is infected, then around the champignon every week everything should be sprayed with a 4% formalin solution. And after each break, it is necessary to spray the shoulders with a 1% solution of copper sulfate. The infected substrate is also treated with a 1% solution of copper sulphate and only then taken to landfill. This substrate cannot be used as an organic fertilizer. After each crop rotation, all production facilities must be steamed for 12 hours at a temperature of 72°C.

What to do if confetti mold appears on mushrooms

Confetti yellow mold is a different disease from normal yellow mold. It is caused by another type of parasitic fungus. A whitish mycelium forms in the substrate in the form of scattered spots. It turns yellow a little later and then turns yellow-brown. In between, fungal tissue can even form.

Developed simultaneously with the champignon mycelium, this parasite gradually begins to prevail. The points can be clearly seen through the bag. They are also easy to check by pouring the substrate from the bag onto paper and dividing it into horizontal layers. The mold is usually different from that of the champignon mycelium in color - it is always silver-gray. It has a depressive effect on the fruiting of champignons. First it slows down, then it stops.

The maximum development of mold occurs in the 50-60th day after sowing the mycelium. Therefore, the later fruiting comes in the champignon, the greater the losses.

The spores of this moldy parasitic fungus die at temperatures of 60°C and above. Most often the disease spreads through the substrate, sometimes it can even be found on the ground. Infection can enter the substrate when it is discharged. The spores are carried by the wind along with dust from nearby fungi or waste substrate. Soil material can also be infected. Disputes are carried along with clothes and shoes, with tools, ticks, mice, mushroom flies, etc.

To prevent infection, it is necessary to comply with sanitary requirements both in the champignon itself and in the adjacent territory. Composting must not be done on an earth floor. The substrate must be pasteurized correctly for 12 hours at a temperature of 60°C. It is preferable to use bags of polymer film, which will reduce the risk of spreading the infection when sewing champignons. In addition, all measures must be strictly carried out (preparation of a selection substrate, rapid germination of the mycelium, mixing with a pasteurized substrate and others) that accelerate the growth of the mycelium and the formation of fruits. This will help reduce the risk of crop loss.

The main measures to combat mold fungi are preventative. First of all, it is necessary to remove all sources of infection at all stages of mushroom cultivation.

In order for mold not to appear on mushrooms, it is necessary to spray the entire area around the champignons once a week with a 1% solution of copper sulfate. Before removing it from the champignon, the substrate must be treated with a solution of copper sulphate. It can be used as an organic fertilizer only where there are no champignons. Production facilities also need to be steamed with the substrate.

Yellow green mushroom mold

Yellow green mold affects the substrate in mushrooms quite often. The mushrooms become weak, gray in color; the mycelium is gradually dying. In its place, moldy fungi with yellow-green spores and whitish mycelium are formed. It has a distinctive musty smell and feels viscous. This disease is caused by several different molds. They are able to develop at the same time, and isolating them is quite difficult. This type of mold is common in nature. It enters the substrate together with the starting materials and, together with other microorganisms, participates in composting. Yellow-green mold begins to develop at a temperature of 45°C. It dies completely with good pasteurization. If pasteurization is done badly and the substrate itself is of poor quality, mold quickly affects the mushroom mycelium in the early stages of development. Infection can penetrate a quality substrate. Sources of infection can be the substrate, or infected waste, which is scattered near the site of champignons and compost, wind and dust, shoes, tools. It is too late to think about what to do when the mushrooms are already moldy. If the infection occurs in a relatively late period, when the mycelium has fully formed and fruit formation has begun, the risk of crop loss is slightly reduced.

To prevent this disease, you must always follow all the rules of hygiene on the compost site. Do not use long-stored bird droppings. Composting must be carried out, adhering to all requirements and placing it in the shoulder area. The substrate must always be heat treated. In addition, it must be moistened immediately after extracting the mushroom from it. On windy days, it is not recommended to clean it. The spent substrate must be removed in plastic bags. Wash the mushrooms regularly and disinfect with fungicides.

Other types of mold fungi

Carmine mold caused by the mildew fungus Sporendomena purpurescens. It appears during fruiting in the form of white down or a mycelium cover between lumps of integumentary material. The mycelium of this mold develops very quickly and covers the entire layer of lining material. It does not absorb water during irrigation. In champignons, fruiting first decreases, then stops altogether. The mold mycelium turns yellow, then turns cherry red and spore formation begins. This mushroom is very fond of nitrogen and grows in a substrate rich in it. If the temperature of the substrate becomes 10-18°C, the growth of the mold fungus increases, and the development of the cultivated fungus, on the contrary, slows down.

To prevent this disease, a substrate that is oversaturated with nitrogen and flooded with water should be avoided. Very carefully, nitrogen fertilizers must be applied. During the heat treatment of the substrate, there must certainly be an inflow of fresh air. Ammonia must be completely released. The substrate temperature must also always be optimal for the cultivated mushroom.

Spider web and olive mold - the most common diseases of the oyster mushroom. They appear on the substrate and inhibit mycelium growth and fruit formation. The simplest and most effective way to combat these diseases is salt. It is usually sprinkled over infected areas. Salt does not allow the disease to spread further.

Growing mushrooms is not a particularly difficult activity. However, it is essential to operate in a sterile and perfectly clean environment.

A single mold spore can contaminate substrate, jars, or equipment and can destroy an entire crop of fungi. Read on to find out how contamination occurs, how to spot it, and how to prevent it.

If your mushroom grow has been contaminated, distinctive signs usually (but not always) appear. These symptoms differ according to the type of fungus or bacterium that has contaminated the crop.

• MELMA

Various types of bacteria can attack the fungus crop. In these cases the mycelium or the grain take on a slimy consistency. A sort of mud develops mainly on the areas where the substrate presses against the glass. Yellow or brown colored slime rings may also appear around the grain. Sometimes, the colony of bacteria can form a scab or gel-like substance on the surface.

• ATYPICAL SMELLS

Not all contamination is necessarily visible to the naked eye. Sometimes, a suspicious smell can signal that something has gone wrong with your mushroom plantation. An unusual odor can be useful in identifying contamination if the contaminant looks the same as the mycelium. Inspect your substrate for any musty, stale smells and any odors other than mushrooms.

• DISCOLORATION

Thankfully, many types of molds have distinctive pigmentation, which makes them very easy to spot. Look for typical mold colors, which can be greenish, blue, white, gray, or black, depending on the type of fungus.

• FRAGMENTATION

When your mushroom grow is contaminated with harmful

spores, it means that two types of mushrooms are growing in your substrate at the same time. Since these two mushrooms are in competition with each other, you should typically notice sharp boundaries separating the two mycelia. This phenomenon is called fragmentation.

So try to promptly identify the areas where the substrate appears separated from the rest of the crop.

• SPOROPHORES

Sporophores are the thin, filamentous structures of a fungus. They may not initially be visible to the naked eye, as they are very small. Some sporophores are larger, and if so, you may notice them. With a magnifying glass it will be easier to spot these long whisker-like fibers, with a small "bubble" at the end.

• UNUSUAL SMOOTH AND SPONGY MYCELIA

Some types of mold can form very dense mycelium. If you are growing them in a jar, this unwelcome fungus can spread quickly and occupy the entire volume of the container. In this case it will be easy to notice the spongy and smooth aspect of the mycelium, very different from the normal mycelium of hallucinogenic mushrooms.

• PULVISCULAR CONSISTENCY

Many types of fungi can be difficult to spot with the naked eye, but a magnifying glass can make it easier to find. Sporophores of fungi often form a dust-like layer on the surface of the mycelium. With a magnifying glass, you can clearly distinguish this "fungal dust" from the rest of the substrate, and from any harmless discolorations of the mycelium.

• SOFT WHITE PATCHES (OVERLAPPING)

When the substrate is contaminated, the infected area can appear soft, sticky and crumbly. These softer areas appear on the surface of the mycelium and, due to their whitish color, are clearly distinguishable from the rest of the substrate.

TYPES OF CONTAMINATING MUSHROOMS

Kinds Of Contaminating Mushrooms

• PENICILLIO (P. CHRYSOGENUM, P. EXPANSUM)

Penicillium is the most common type of mold in the world. Penicillium spores spread through the air and can easily contaminate your substrate. The mold then propagates in the jar, rapidly expanding until it infects the entire mycelium of the fungi.

Penicillium contamination is initially white in color, and it can be difficult to distinguish from normal mushroom mycelium. Penicillium colonies have a circular shape. Penicillium often develops on wood. Fortunately, Penicillium rarely contaminates the spores to be inoculated. In most cases, contamination occurs on the grain not yet colonized. Penicillium gives off a musty and dirty smell.

• ASPERGILLO

Aspergillus fungus is another very common fungus that spreads through the air and can infect your crop. The mycelium of the

Aspergillus has a light gray color, very similar to the mycelium. Some Aspergillus species can be yellow, black, green, brown, or blue, or can take on multiple shades. Sometimes, Aspergillus colonies form a ring, with a denser mycelium layer at the edges. Aspergillus has a slimy, musty smell.

- TRICODERMA (T. VIRIDE, T. HARZIANUM, T. KONINGII)

Just like Penicillium and Aspergillus, Trichoderma is a very common contaminating fungus. It is a particularly aggressive species, responsible for the destruction of countless crops. The mycelium of Trichoderma takes on a grayish tinge, not always easy to identify. Spores can transfer to the substrate via soil, dust or contaminated clothing. When the infection is already in place, a dense white layer appears on the surface. Trichoderma spores can produce a yellowish or green mycelium, and the colony is bordered by a whitish ring.

Tricoderma contamination can occur at any stage of cultivation. Unfortunately, it can be difficult to notice the infection early, as sporulation can occur later, after inoculation. For this reason, mushroom growers should check the odor emanating from the mycelium, to detect the presence of mold and prevent it from spreading. Unfortunately, not all types of Trichoderma mushrooms have a characteristic smell. However, some emit an aroma similar to that of coconut.

- BACILLO (B. SUBTILIS, B. CEREUS)

Bacillus is not a fungus, but a type of bacterium. However, it is a very dangerous and common contaminant in mushroom crops. The heat-resistant B. subtilis is the most widespread species. The presence of this bacterium manifests itself as a sort of crust or slimy area on the substrate. Contamination occurs mainly from inadequately sterilized equipment. The risk of infection is greater when inoculation syringes are stored at temperatures above ambient temperatures. You can identify Bacillus contamination by the foul, rotting smell emitted by this bacterium.

• MUCOR (CAT HAIR)

The "cat hair" mold is so called because of its thin filaments (sporophores), with small heads at the end. It is a contaminating mold that can attack the spores of inoculated fungi, but rarely grows on the substrate.

• RHIZOPUS (R. STOLONIFERA, R. ORYZAE)

Rhizopus is another contaminant. It is a very difficult mold to manage because it can spread very quickly. It has a "cat's hair" mold-like appearance, with long, hair-like strands, with a rounded tip. Rhizopus has an acrid odor, which sometimes resembles that of alcohol.

• YEASTS

Yeasts are another very common contaminant and, just like fungi and bacteria, they can destroy an entire crop. The presence of yeast is manifested by small spots inside the jar, usually yellow or white.

Some types of yeast can resemble bacterial contamination. Usually yeasts do not attack substrates, but they may be present in the spores to be inoculated. The yeasts give off various odors.

So far we have listed just a few of the major contaminants that can affect your mushroom growing. Many other types of organisms, including fungi, bacteria and yeasts, can attack your valuable crop or, at best, severely limit your final yield. You certainly don't want this to happen. Here are some tips to avoid fungal contamination.

HOW TO AVOID CONTAMINATION OF MUSHROOMS

If you want to successfully grow mushrooms, avoiding dangerous contamination, the fundamental rule is to always work in a sterilized environment and follow strict hygiene procedures. In most cases, a single harmful spore or bacterium is enough to contaminate the entire mushroom crop. Hobby growers do not usually operate in a 100% sterile environment, such as a laboratory. However, there are some strategies to minimize the risk of contamination.

Sterile Growing Environment

Many contaminants such as molds and fungi spread through the air. They can be anywhere, even in seemingly clean spaces, and you can't see them. Therefore, eliminating these harmful molecules can be complicated. In professional laboratories, scientists use special filtered air booths called laminar flow hoods. Unfortunately, this particular piece of equipment is very expensive, and certainly out of reach for an occasional mushroom grower. On the other hand, though, if you love DIY, you might be able to build a semi-professional laminar flow hood with your own hands.

Alternatively, you can use an SAB (airtight box). An SAB is not as sophisticated as a laminar flow hood, but it can still provide a clean enough environment for growing mushrooms. An SAB is basically a box with two side holes in which to insert your hands. You can sterilize the inside walls of this "miniature laboratory", and work on your beloved mushrooms by inserting your hands into the holes.

STERILIZE SUBSTRATE AND WHEAT

Airborne contaminating molecules are a big problem. But often they are already present also in the substrate. Many substrates and bulk cereals contain unwanted organisms, which must be eliminated or at least minimized before use. Therefore, you must sterilize both the substrate and the grain before inoculating the mushroom spores.

You can sterilize blocks of sawdust and wheat grains using a pressure cooker, large enough to hold all the material. Place the block of sawdust in the pot and sterilize it for about 2 and a half hours. For the wheat, 1 hour and a half will suffice.

Sterilization is a procedure that removes all types of bacteria. Pasteurization is another method that uses heat to remove most of the bacteria. Pasteurization is not adequate for sanitizing sawdust blocks, but it is a good technique if you use straw as a substrate. To pasteurize the straw, heat it to 65–82°C for at least an hour and a half. Some growers put the straw in a pot full of water, and then put it to heat on a stove.

TRY TO STAY CLEAN WHILE WORKING WITH MUSHROOMS

We now know what the factors are that can contaminate the environment, the air and the substrate. But we have not yet considered the main source of contamination: yourself!

Your clothes, skin, and hair can act as carriers for contaminants. To grow mushrooms in the best possible conditions, personal hygiene is essential.

Before working on your mushrooms, take a shower and wash your hair. We are not talking about a quick shower. Rub the skin well, wash thoroughly also under the nails and behind the ears, and in any other area of the body. Hand sanitizers can be very helpful in eliminating bacteria on the skin.

In professional laboratories, operators wear a lab coat. You probably won't have such a sterilized uniform available, but you should still use clean clothes before you start working on your grow. It is also advisable to wear a mask.

USE STERILIZED TOOLS

Obviously, it makes no sense to work in a perfectly clean environment if sterilized instruments are not used. In other words, you need to sanitize all equipment and utensils such as scalpels, blades and syringes.

When using the scalpel for transfers, you must absolutely

remember to sterilize it. To do this, heat it over a flame for about 30 seconds, until it turns red. You can use a Bunsen burner or an alcohol lamp. If you have nothing else available, a lighter is fine too.

Clearly, you cannot heat syringes and plastic instruments over a flame. In this case, you have to use alcohol to sterilize them.

Alcohol is also useful for cleaning all surfaces, including jars and bags. A couple of bottles of denatured (isopropyl) alcohol and a few sheets of paper towels will allow you to keep your workspace clean and disinfected.

CONTAMINATION OF MUSHROOMS

Perhaps you will not be able to achieve a degree of sterilization of 100% in the environment predisposed to the inoculation of mushrooms. After all, contaminants like bacteria and fungi can be found anywhere, anytime. But, with the tips in this guide, you will certainly be able to minimize the risk of contamination

CHAPTER 21

HOW TO DO BUSINESS WITH SHIITAKE MUSHROOMS

What started out as a hobby has now grown into a profitable business.

I enjoyed eating mushrooms every day and explored how to grow shiitake mushrooms in my home.

However, since I have been doing this for some time and am now enjoying my hobby, I will explain to you how you too can grow and start earning from your efforts.

For shiitake farming then, I suggest you learn the basics of log inoculation and the maintenance and fruiting of your logs. Also, to get started, you can buy a shiitake kit or a pre-cut log to try it out at home.

So, if you are ready to go further, let's understand how to sell shiitake mushrooms as a business.

Even though the logs can produce 5 pounds or more of shiitake , they mostly do so over a period of 2 to 3 years. So, to get a decent weekly harvest, you will need lots of logs and a regular commitment to start new ones.

Finally, you need to do research with local, regional and federal authorities to find out the legal conditions for selling shiitake mushrooms where you live.

If you are willing to do all this work, then let me share some secrets on how to make a profit selling shiitake.

4 ways to sell your mushrooms

Here are some ideas to consider for selling shiitake mushrooms.

1. Agricultural markets

Farmers' markets are a good outlet for selling shiitake mushrooms. In general, it is possible to charge twice as much for well-packaged mushrooms in the market than for bulk packaged mushrooms. Prices can vary between 12 and 20 euros in some regions.

Unfortunately, mushrooms have been a popular product on the agricultural market for several years. For example, the more established, high-income farmers' markets are often already saturated with mushroom vendors. Also, in newer or lower-income markets, it can be difficult to charge full price for mushrooms and there may not be enough customer interest to sell them every week.

Markets also take a long time, between preparing things, setting up the stand, staying at the event and returning home. Time spent and special equipment required, such as coolers, ice packs, signage, packaging, tables, umbrellas, gas, etc. can reduce the potential profit from the sale of shiitake.

If you already have a stand at the market for other reasons, such as selling handicrafts and vegetables, adding mushrooms can be a great way to complement your product line and make extra profits.

2. sell shiitake mushrooms to restaurants

Selling to restaurants is another way to make money from shiitake. If you live near an upscale place, with restaurants that are committed to buying local produce, you can also get a good deal by selling only to restaurants.

However, be aware that it is much easier for chefs and purchasing managers to work with large distributors who can meet all their needs with one delivery and one invoice. So frankly, the kind of chefs and restaurant staff who are willing to work with local food producers do so for ethical and community reasons.

It will therefore be necessary to invest some time in developing a relationship, for example by collaborating on community events to raise awareness of local food movements. Also, as chefs are already taking longer to source locally, make sure you stick to your schedule.

Deliver on time every week. Make sure you can fulfill orders before accepting them. In other words, put an extra effort into ensuring the long-term success of your shiitake sales.

3. wholesaling to distributors

These first two methods are ideal for anyone planning to spend a lot of time developing a shiitake business, but if you are a farmer and are looking to make a little more money by increasing what you do for homemade food production, there is another option.

Wholesaling to a distributor is easier. Distributors come in many forms, so you may need to do some research to find one near you.

- Food centers and cooperatives

Large retailers, such as those that work with supermarkets and restaurant chains, often need larger quantities of goods than a small producer can supply. However, thanks to the local food movement, there are now cooperatives and feeding centers that allow many small producers to group their products together and serve the larger farms.

Check with your local agriculture or extension office to find out if there are any food centers or cooperatives offering energy sharing opportunities in your area.

- Mushroom dealers

Sometimes other mushroom retailers have higher demand for shiitake than they can reasonably supply on a regular basis. Mushroom dealers can also be attached to things that can grow quickly on substrates like oyster straw or lion's mane. They cannot grow shiitake on logs and will benefit from being able to add your shiitake to their range of mushrooms.

Through wholesaling to other local growers

Resellers who already have an established customer base benefit from your network without having to make all the deliveries.

You will earn less money per pound on this side. However, it can be even more affordable when you consider the time spent and other expenses like car maintenance, gas, stress, packaging, and even more so for markets or direct sales to restaurants.

4. Value-added products

One last way to make money with shiitake is to make value-added products. Dried shiitake mushrooms are very popular, as is shiitake powder and shiitake seasoning mix. All of them get high prices in farmer's markets and through online retailers.

There are generally more legal obstacles to the sale of packaged products. A kitchen inspection may be required. There will likely be labeling requirements. In addition, higher taxes generally have to be paid for a prepared product than for the sale of a raw mushroom treated as a product.

Thankfully, you don't have to worry about your shiitake deteriorating. Raw shiitakes only last a few weeks, even if they are stored properly at around 4°C, in a moderately humid space. By producing dry products, you can keep shiitake much longer and reduce product loss. You can also sell shiitake that look less attractive in powder form.

You can also focus your sales efforts on holidays, when people tend to spend more on luxury items instead of going to the market every week. If you don't like leaving the house, try internet sales as well. Before committing a crime, make sure you have the legal rights to sell shiitake mushrooms across national or state borders!

How to effectively grow shiitake for profit

Now, if you are ready to start growing shiitake for profit using the ideas above, or whatever other ideas you may have, then there are a few things to consider when moving from home production to professional distribution.

Step 1: reduce costs

For domestic production, using pre-made shiitake caps is an inexpensive way to start and have a successful first crop. However, if you need to inoculate hundreds of registers each year for production, you may want to make some improvements to your processes.

First, move on to sawdust seeds for inoculation. It is much cheaper and easier to use if you have the right tools. You will need an inoculation tool to use it. But this one-time investment will pay for itself in the first year.

Step 2: Add efficiency

You also want to make sure you have the right tools to inoculate all those magazines. Create an inoculation table with wheels that allow the logs to be rotated 360 degrees without moving them. Also, upgrade the drill with a drill bit to drill spawning holes faster.

When using these specialized tools you can inoculate an entire log in minutes while standing comfortably at a table built for your height.

Step 3: Organize the production line

As shiitake production reaches increasing levels, a large enough "spawning yard" (the official term for where logs are kept) is needed. Your yard can be on the edge of a forest, the north side of your home, under a shed or a shaded tarp, or even indoors. However, no matter where you install it, make sure it is well organized.

In general, you should organize your logs based on when they are most likely to fruit. Different strains adapted to cold, heat and diversity will have different fruiting times.

- Broad spectrum strains

Wide range strains are the simplest and most reliable for forcing fruit to around 10-25°C. They are often a mainstay for anyone looking to get fruit on a schedule and get quick shiitake production. They usually need the largest area in a forecourt for shiitake placement.

You can dip and force fruit into your large logs every 8 weeks. By dividing the logs into 8 batches of fruit in your yard, you can work the yard one week of logs at a time. Then, when you get to the end of the line, you start all over again!

Shiitake culture indoors?

Shiitake culture is becoming more and more popular. People use polytunnels and greenhouses for production. Some also use workshops, basements and sheds.

When grown indoors, you have greater temperature control and can achieve year-round production. However, more work needs to be done to water the logs and provide the equivalent of sunlight for colonization and maintenance of the logs.

Misting systems and electric daytime running lights may be required for indoor production. Don't forget that the logs need to be watered, so drainage will also be essential.

In our temperate climate, it is easier for us to colonize our outdoor logs in wooded areas. However, when the logs start to stick together, we get the prettiest shiitake blankets if we put them away. This protects the caps from excessive rainfall and minimizes the risk of insect damage.

How to move forward

It is only necessary to plant once a year, but it is possible to harvest for several years once the logs start producing.

As long as your logs come from freshly felled trees and you inoculate them before they warm up, the chances of competing fungi colonizing your logs are minimal.

- The life of your logs

Your logs will take 6 to 18 months to colonize depending on the shiitake strain used and its condition. Thereafter, the logs tend to produce their maximum yield during the first two years of use.

Unforced fruit logs last longer. Depending on the size of the trunk, they can last from 3 to 5 years and continue to bear fruit in season.

- Annual inoculation

For continuous production, inoculate the logs with resistant strains. Then complete your seasonal cover by inoculating the logs every two years with cold strains.

Move old logs to orchards or shady areas to decompose and enrich the soil, occasionally offering shiitake crops until completely rotted.

This can still be a great way to make a small profit from something you already grow for your own use, even if you're a mushroom fanatic and enjoy eating mushrooms every day!

www.ingramcontent.com/pod-product-compliance
Lightning Source LLC
Chambersburg PA
CBHW070632030426
42337CB00020B/3992